TWO MINUTES IN THE BIBLE®

THROUGH

Revelation

BOYD BAILEY

HARVEST HOUSE PUBLISHERS
EUGENE, OREGON

Cover design by Bryce Williamson

Cover Image © borchee / iStock

TWO MINUTES IN THE BIBLE is a trademark of Boyd Bailey. Harvest House Publishers, Inc., is the exclusive licensee of the trademark TWO MINUTES IN THE BIBLE.

TWO MINUTES IN THE BIBLE® THROUGH REVELATION
Copyright © 2018 Boyd Bailey
Published by Harvest House Publishers
Eugene, Oregon 97408
www.harvesthousepublishers.com

ISBN 978-0-7369-6927-7 (pbk.)
ISBN 978-0-7369-6928-4 (eBook)

Library of Congress Cataloging-in-Publication Data

Names: Bailey, Boyd, 1960- author.
Title: Two minutes in the Bible through Revelation / Boyd Bailey.
Description: Eugene, Oregon : Harvest House Publishers, 2018.
Identifiers: LCCN 2017029357 (print) | LCCN 2017048382 (ebook) | ISBN 9780736969284 (ebook) | ISBN 9780736969277 (pbk.)
Subjects: LCSH: Bible. Revelation—Meditations.
Classification: LCC BS2825.54 (ebook) | LCC BS2825.54 .B35 2018 (print) | DDC 228/.06—dc23
LC record available at https://lccn.loc.gov/2017029357

Printed in the United States of America

17 18 19 20 21 22 23 24 25 26 / VP-CD / 10 9 8 7 6 5 4 3 2 1

To Jess and Angela Correll
who inspire all of us
with their BIG vision of God
and what He can do

Acknowledgments

Thank you, Butch and Teresa Ferguson, for teaching me as a new Christian about the second coming of Christ. Your influence during my senior year of high school facilitated my faith in Jesus!

Thank you, Wisdom Hunters team, for loving like Jesus: Rita Bailey, Bethany Thoms, Gwynne Maffett, Shana Schutte, Rachel Snead, Rachel Prince, Tripp Prince, Susan Fox, and Josh Randolph.

Thank you, Susan Fox and Gene Skinner, for your expert editing.

Thank you, Wisdom Hunters board of directors, for your love, prayers, and accountability: Jack McEntee, Cliff Bartow, Andrew Wexler, and John Hightower.

Thank you, National Christian Foundation, for the opportunity, by God's grace, to reach and restore every person by the love of Christ, and to mobilize biblical generosity for God's kingdom.

Thank you, Harvest House Publishers, for your vision and support for this book—especially to Bob Hawkins, Terry Glaspey, Gene Skinner, Ken Lorenz, Kathy Zemper, and Brad Moses.

Introduction

⌾⌾⌾

We hosted a "reveal party" at our home for our daughter and son-in-law's baby because none of us, except the expecting parents, knew the gender. It was a festive occasion, full of joyful anticipation. Everyone chose one of two sides—the baby-blue decoration on the left or the precious pink on the right—as our friend Donna was perched on the deck above with camera in hand, ready to capture the raw emotion of the moment. JT and Bethany pulled the trigger on a gun-like contraption that launched a brilliant Roman-candle display of blue confetti all over the backyard. Five of us on the boy side were ecstatic, and the fifteen or so on the girl side were equally berserk. There was no pique, only jubilation at the revelation of this hope, soon to become reality—the birth of a firstborn!

The book of Revelation is all about Jesus Christ and His reveal party—His salvation, His faithfulness, His judgment, His heaven, and His second coming. Joining Him on this breathtaking journey are His faithful followers, who repent and persevere during intense persecution, awaiting the fulfillment of His promise of a heavenly future. Sadly, there are also the unfaithful who deny Christ. They are drawn into Satan's deadly schemes and will occupy hell for eternity.

With mind-blowing emotion, Jesus reveals Himself to His beloved disciple John in a flurry of visions pronouncing His kingship and lordship over all creation—the good and the bad, the beautiful and the ugly, the believers and unbelievers, the Spirit-led and the devil-deceived. In the end, Jesus promises to come again quickly and to provide abundant grace in the interim.

Though Revelation can be a head-scratcher with its symbolism and strange imagery, these prophetic writings warm my heart with their heavenly focus on praise and worship of Jesus. As I read, the Spirit moves my soul to wait with urgent obedience, and He compels me to share the gospel with all tribes and tongues worldwide. Yes, the Lord Jesus Christ, revealed in all His majestic glory, calls forth my commitment to not grow weary in well-doing and to remain faithful to bring Him my sacrifice of praise—especially when my feelings belie my beliefs. Revelation is more than a reminder of my reigning Lord's kingship—He is also my ever-present strength, empowering me to humbly serve in His kingdom and gladly give Him all glory!

What about the passages in Revelation that are unclear at best and confusing at worst? As with other challenging verses in the Bible, we first interpret the God-breathed Word by comparing it with other scriptural passages, and when we do, we discover a consistent imprint of Old Testament influence and Holy Spirit inspiration. Then we prayerfully seek to apply New Testament understanding to the text. The much-loved apostle John received his revelation from Jesus in the context of his contemporary culture and his comprehension of sacred Jewish Scripture. If we read aloud the words written in Revelation and take them to heart, we can be sure we will be blessed (1:3) so we can be a blessing.

We are waiting on Jesus and His return, not in worrisome dread, but in a celebration of joyful anticipation. Revelation shows us our Savior Jesus in His regal power so we can worship Him, trust Him, love Him, obey Him, and rest in Him. So now and in the end—by His grace—we can confidently say, "Even so, come quickly, Lord Jesus."

Expectantly awaiting Jesus's return,
Boyd Bailey
Roswell, Georgia

1

Grace and Peace

—⚮—

*Grace and peace to you…from Jesus Christ, who
is the faithful witness, the firstborn from the
dead, and the ruler of the kings of the earth.*

REVELATION 1:4-5

Grace and peace are gifts from God that every human heart craves. Grace for sustaining strength during sickness and peace in the process. Grace for continued forgiveness in a challenging relationship and peace that produces patience. Grace for ongoing gratitude and peace when things don't go our way. Grace for generous giving and peace in God's faithful provision. A heart governed by grace and peace is a heart filled with the Lord's love. Grace and peace come from Jesus.

John is secluded in exile, and his Lord had ascended to heaven decades earlier. Yet in some ways, John sees Jesus more clearly in this vision than he did when they were together. Jesus Christ is the faithful witness who gives His children grace and peace. How? In His words and His actions, Jesus revealed who God is—the loving heavenly Father. Jesus's sonship gave His story veracity, so He stated the facts with humble authority. Jesus testifies to truth, and His reassuring words extend grace and peace.

—⚮—

"The reason I was born and came into the
world is to testify to the truth. Everyone on the
side of truth listens to me" (John 18:37).

Grace and peace come to those who believe Jesus is the firstborn from the dead. Others, like Lazarus, died and were brought back to life, but they died again. Jesus Christ is the only one whose body was transformed in resurrection power, never to experience death again. Faith in the resurrection is essential if we are to receive the Lord's grace and peace. We cannot remove the supernatural from Jesus and just keep the natural. Trust in Christ's resurrection is the key that unlocks the treasure chest of riches found in His grace and peace. Those who would embrace Jesus must embrace His miracles. These hugs from heaven warm our hearts by His loving care.

Tranquility comes to hearts that trust in Christ as their Lord. Crown Him conqueror over death, and you will enjoy His grace and peace while dying. Crown Him Lord over fear, and you will receive His grace and peace while afraid. Crown Him all-wise King and learn how to make the best decisions. Crown Him Lord over sin and apply His grace and peace when in need of forgiveness. Whatever we face, Christ has already faced—and has overcome. Thus, we come to the One who is full of grace and peace!

⸎

"[To those] who have been chosen according to
the foreknowledge of God the Father, through the
sanctifying work of the Spirit, to be obedient to
Jesus Christ and sprinkled with his blood: Grace
and peace be yours in abundance" (1 Peter 1:2).

Whom or what do I need to entrust to Jesus? Have I received His grace and peace?

Related Readings
Psalm 89:27; Isaiah 55:4; Romans 1:7; 1 Timothy 6:15; 2 John 3

2

Liberated by Love

———— ∽∾ ————

To him who loves us and has freed
us from our sins by his blood.

REVELATION 1:5

As a 19-year-old freshman in college, I was shackled by my sins. I felt chained to my past pain, held captive by my present guilt, and fearful of the future consequences of my misdeeds. Fortunately, I was introduced to the love of God by a godly family whose evangelism was love—love for each other and for me. They invited me to church, where I understood for the first time the seriousness of my sins and the abundance of God's grace. I trusted in Jesus to save me.

The blood of Christ on the cross not only washes away the stain of our sins; it also breaks the bondage of sin's control over our being. Our lustful thoughts become thoughts of true love. Our desire for more money transforms into quiet generosity. The Holy Spirit tames our angry outbursts into a spirit of gentle patience. Jesus loved us, loves us, and will love us. Our exalted Christ in heaven loves us now, just as He loved us when living as a humble servant on earth. Each nail driven into the cross resounded emancipation. His shed blood liberates us.

———— ∽∾ ————

"How much more, then, will the blood
of Christ…cleanse our consciences from
acts that lead to death, so that we may
serve the living God" (Hebrews 9:14).

Are you held back by a besetting sin? If so, release it to the love of Jesus. His loving forgiveness will heal your malady and replace it with His righteous strength. Sin is an affront to Almighty God not only because of His holiness but also because of His great love. Rejecting divine love says the fleeting affections of one's little idols are enough. Accepting divine love ensures we will always desire eternity's embrace. Your compassionate Lord looks down in empathy and extends His love to you. Will you let go of your trinkets and trust Jesus? His love liberates.

Live in ongoing worshipful celebration of Christ's love, as if you were in a postwar victory parade. Jesus has overcome sin, Satan, and death. We are more than conquerors because Jesus has conquered, is conquering, and will conqueror. He rode a lowly donkey on the road to forgiveness, but He will emerge from heaven mounted on a mighty stallion, ready to judge. The victorious love of Christ flows from hearts full of Him. Believe in and receive the love of Jesus.

"In all these things we are more than conquerors through him who loved us" (Romans 8:37).

What distorted love of mine needs Christ's perfect love? What controlling sin do I need to be freed of?

Related Readings
Romans 5:8-9; Galatians 2:20; Ephesians 1:7; 5:2; 1 Peter 1:18-20

3

Kings and Priests

[He] has made us kings and priests to His God and Father,
to Him be glory and dominion forever and ever. Amen.

REVELATION 1:6 NKJV

A humbling thought: By faith in Jesus, He makes us kings, queens, and priests. We are to reign with Him in His future kingdom, but also we reign with Christ now. We have dominion over ourselves and the world around us. When we bow to our Master Jesus, He empowers us to master the good and the bad in our lives. Jesus became the Son of Man so we could become sons and daughters of the Most High. Christ became like us so we could grow into His likeness.

What does it mean for us to have dominion over ourselves? We can overcome unrighteousness. We are no longer slaves to sin since our righteous Savior overcame death. We rule over sin because our Ruler won the fight against evil forces. When we live in defeat, we are like prisoners of war who remain in the enemy camp even though the prison doors are unlocked and wide open. Not only have we been set free from sin, self, and Satan; now we rule over them. We are royalty!

"For everyone born of God overcomes the
world. This is the victory that has overcome
the world, even our faith" (1 John 5:4).

Why has Jesus made His followers priests? He made us priests because He was the great High Priest who sacrificed Himself for our sins (Hebrews 9:11-12). Our priesthood means we have direct access to our heavenly Father. We lift up our offerings of praise, thanksgiving, and repentance to Him. We bring our sacrifices to God since Christ sacrificed His life for us. Every follower of Jesus is a priest who daily surrenders and points people to Jesus. Priests mediate for God.

How can you use your royal priesthood for the advancement of God's kingdom? Prayerfully develop your professional platform. Mold your culture after the gospel of Christ through excellent work, collaboration, and compassion. Maybe you engage insiders in the faith and outsiders in Bible study, prayer, or fun outings. It may mean becoming more involved in your children's education to have increased influence over their spiritual and material roles in the world. Invite friends to church so they can learn how to have a friend in Jesus. A royal priesthood governs with grace.

"But you are a chosen people, a royal priesthood, a holy nation, God's special possession, that you may declare the praises of him who called you out of darkness into his wonderful light" (1 Peter 2:9).

How can I better govern my life for God? With whom can I share the gospel of Jesus?

Related Readings
Exodus 19:6; Isaiah 62:12; John 16:33; Colossians 1:12-14; Hebrews 4:14-16

4

Tribulation in Christ

―――⊷∞⊶―――

*I, John, your brother and companion in the tribulation
and kingdom and patient endurance which are in Jesus...*

REVELATION 1:9 AMP

Followers of Jesus travel along paths of inevitable tribulation (trouble). As citizens of God's kingdom, our life in Christ invites trials. Jesus is very clear: In Him we will suffer persecution. Those who embrace the world are not a threat to the world, but those who are ruled by Christ will rule with Christ—not just later, but now. Righteous rulers are cause for the unrighteous to be uncomfortable, and adversaries of Jesus seek to discredit His followers. Since Jesus suffered unjust accusations, we can expect the same. Tribulations test our faithfulness.

John writes as a fellow partaker of suffering for Christ's sake. He had matured beyond his early days of seeking kingdom power for selfish motives, and after submitting to King Jesus, he had become a Spirit-filled servant of the Lord. Exiled by his persecutors to isolation and virtual martyrdom, he remained true to the Word of God and the testimony of Jesus Christ. Since by faith he sided with his Savior, John had all he needed. The best adversity is an adversity not wasted on fear.

―――⊷∞⊶―――

"If you are insulted because of the name of
Christ, you are blessed, for the Spirit of glory
and of God rests on you" (1 Peter 4:14).

What blessings are behind your tribulation? Perhaps unfair allegations are drawing you closer to Christ. Persecution flushes out false faith and validates genuine trust in God. Because of your bold belief in Jesus, you may be labeled narrow-minded—even bigoted—but you know in your heart that God's love motivates you. Integrity may cost you; if so, remain humble, knowing you suffer reproach for the sake of the gospel. Christ's followers are partakers of Christ's suffering. Blessings come when we suffer for His sake.

How can we patiently endure tribulation as active citizens in God's kingdom? One way is to support fellow followers of Jesus who have been exiled for their faith. We can become a refuge of help, healing, and hope. Soldiers of the faith need our assistance when they are wounded by the world. During persecution we stay faithful to the Word of God and to the testimony of Jesus Christ—His death for our sin and His resurrection. Persecution is our chance as true believers to overcome untruths with our love.

"You will be counted worthy of the kingdom of God,
for which you are suffering" (2 Thessalonians 1:5).

How can I patiently endure trials? Who is suffering persecution today, and how can I help that person?

Related Readings
John 15:21; Romans 8:18; 2 Corinthians 1:5; 1 Peter 5:1,10; Revelation 2:10

5

Unified Around Jesus

———◦∞◦———

*I saw seven golden lampstands, and among the
lampstands was someone like a son of man...the
seven lampstands are the seven churches.*

REVELATION 1:12-13,20

Our Christmas candlelight church service is a highlight of our year. Those who have come to faith in Christ over the past 12 months light their candles first. Brilliant lights, each reflecting the salvation of a once darkened soul, sets the worship center aglow. Joyful applause erupts celebrating the Light of Life giving eternal and abundant life to new babes in Christ. Worshipfully, the rest of us who follow Jesus quietly light our candles in honor of our Lord. Unified faith in Christ is a compelling testimony for Him.

The Romans exiled the apostle John to the island of Patmos because of his faith. Now, like Daniel, he has become a prophet. The Lord speaks to him through visions of what had been, what is now, and what is to come. It is sobering and encouraging to see Jesus Christ in all His glory and authority calling churches to be a unified light for Him. Jesus commissioned John to write these prophetic words on a scroll and to send them to the seven churches. John knew if the cross of Jesus was lifted up in our lives and in our churches, all humanity would be drawn to Him.

———◦∞◦———

"When I am lifted up from the earth, then all of
humanity will be drawn to Me" (John 12:32 VOICE).

The world is not moved by a church that looks like the world. What moves the world toward Jesus is a church that looks like another world: one that embraces the cross and the resurrection of Jesus through a community of believers who sacrifice and suffer for their Savior's sake and for each other. In the same way global allies come together to combat a common enemy, so diverse followers of Jesus unify to come against evil forces. Faith unified by Jesus lifts Him up.

Is your faith isolated or engaged? Do you collaborate with other Jesus followers to work together to take the gospel to the world? Christians inclusive of other Christians have more influence with non-Christians. We unite, trusting Jesus as our resurrected Lord and Savior. Perhaps God is calling out His church to repent of proud exclusivity—to not be of the world, but to engage darkness while united by the brilliant light of Christ's gospel.

———— ∞ ————

"There is neither Jew nor Gentile, neither slave
nor free, nor is there male and female, for you
are all one in Christ Jesus" (Galatians 3:28).

What group of Christians can I work with to make society a better place?

Related Readings
Luke 9:49-50; Acts 26:17-18; Colossians 1:12-14; 1 John 1:6; 2:19

6

Life-or-Death Situation

⸺❦⸺

I am the Living One; I was dead, and now look, I am alive
for ever and ever! And I hold the keys of death and Hades.

REVELATION 1:18

We all live in a life-or-death situation. For the elderly, aged by life's elements, death is more imminent. For others, life is just beginning—youthful possibilities pulsate with enviable energy. Still others enter a new reality while battling a terminal illness. The truth is, we are all terminal; but for some, the window in this life is quickly closing. Only as we prepare for death are we really ready for life—and we all need the Lord of Life, Jesus Christ.

Jesus is the Living One. He is the Lord over the living and the dead. The Word (Jesus) became flesh to live among us, and He died to live through us. Faith, without the death and resurrection of Jesus Christ, is only a shell of salvation—not real, but hollow heresy. Jesus holds the keys of death, and He will transform our earthly bodies so they will be like His glorified body (Philippians 3:21). Because Christ is the first and the last, we trust Him in life and in death. We rely on the One who offers us grace for an abundant life and a victorious death.

⸺❦⸺

"Just as sin reigned in death, so also grace might
reign through righteousness to bring eternal life
through Jesus Christ our Lord" (Romans 5:21).

Is death constantly calling on you or a loved one? If so, you have a friend in Jesus to walk with you through the shadows of death's door. Here in your darkest hour is the loving light of your Lord. Let Him guide you by His grace to a good place. God's good place is full of peace and assurance. If you bare your heart and soul, the Holy Spirit will bear your burdens. The prospects of death call forth the prospects of your faith and hope in Christ.

How can we make the most of our lives? Start by engaging Christ as the Lord of your life. Your submission to our Savior Jesus gives you the freedom to enjoy His life expressed through your life. Submission to God means we get under His mission. What is God's mission? To make disciples and to love people—especially those who are difficult to love. In life or death we come alive when we surrender to the Living One: Jesus Christ!

"These are the words of him who is the First and the
Last, who died and came to life again" (Revelation 2:8).

Whom do I know that needs to know Jesus as their living Lord?

Related Readings
Acts 2:24; Romans 6:4; 1 Corinthians 15:43-53

7

Motivation from Revelation

---

*Write, therefore, what you have seen, what
is now and what will take place later.*

REVELATION 1:19

Sometimes I scratch my head while seeking to understand practical applications for my life from the prophetic book of Revelation. The figurative imagery and symbolism can be confusing, even overwhelming. But the more I interpret Scripture with Scripture—and the more I pray over the futuristic words in this last book of the Bible—the more I take to heart God's promises. As I reflect on the perseverance and love of the exiled and elderly disciple John, he challenges me to endure hardships and love radically. Revelation provides a godly motivation!

Verse 19 of chapter 1 gives us a three-part outline of the entire book of Revelation. The first section tells us what John has seen, which is the exalted Christ described in chapter 1. The second section explains "what is now," as John addresses the condition of the seven churches of Asia in chapters 2 and 3. The third and last section of Revelation includes chapters 4 to 22, which cover "what will take place later"—the second coming of Jesus and His millennial reign. Revelation motivates us to focus on Christ glorified and His bride, the church.

"The Lord Himself will descend from heaven
with a shout, with the voice of an archangel, and

with the trumpet of God. And the dead in Christ
will rise first" (1 Thessalonians 4:16 NKJV).

Life today tends to trump life tomorrow, making it difficult to be motivated by events way off in the future. But what if respecting the future could clarify our present circumstances and give us hope to endure? Hope is heaven's remedy for needy souls. Hope in God for peace—not in the troubles of this world. Hope in God for security—not in unreliable economies. Hope in God for forgiveness—not in unmerciful people. Revelation can motivate a life of abundance right now!

We are also compelled to praise the Lord in the glory of His holy majesty when we experience the radical worship graphically and emotionally depicted in Revelation. Here we see Almighty God worshipped for His resounding victory over the enemy. We worship the King of kings and the Lord of lords—not the kings of earth who lord their power and wealth over their citizens. We are motivated to worship because one day we will bow in worship at the Lamb's marriage supper!

"Hallelujah! For our Lord God Almighty
reigns. Let us rejoice and be glad and
give him glory!" (Revelation 19:6-7).

Record in your journal the promises you are trusting God to fulfill.

Related Readings
Genesis 24:48; Isaiah 49:23; 2 Corinthians 1:20; Revelation 15:4

8

Servants of Light

―――――∞――――

*These are the words of him who holds the
seven stars in his right hand and walks
among the seven golden lampstands.*

REVELATION 2:1

My two favorite times of day are sunrise and sunset. The beautiful ball of fire enflames my faith. The warm glow and revealing light reminds me of the gentle, all-encompassing love of my Creator. He reassures me in the morning: "I'm with you today." He gives me rest in the evening, saying, "You can rest in Me." I once lived in darkness—aimless, afraid, and arrogant. But now I live in the light—purposeful, peaceful, and humbled. My allegiance shifted from the master of darkness to the Master of light—the Lord Jesus.

The resurrected Christ walks among the churches providing spiritual direction. He also holds in His right hand the messengers or leaders of the local gathering of believers to direct and protect them. Yes, our Savior and Lord is the source of the churches' power and influence. As the Leader of leaders, He guides them in His will and reveals to them His wisdom. Jesus is absent from us physically but present in the Spirit—as well as in the spirit of His followers.

―――――∞――――

"The true light that gives light to everyone
was coming into the world" (John 1:9).

As Christians we live as light beams of the Lord. Light is invisible, but it has a visible source—the sun. Our light of salvation is invisible, but it points to the visible source of the light—the Son. In a believer's life, any ray of hope, any illumination of wisdom, and any beam of belief comes from the Holy Spirit. The Spirit is our power source. Are you in a dark place—unsure, afraid? Trust in the Lord of light—Jesus.

God's messengers, the leaders in our churches, have the light of Christ to lead them, so they may gently and lovingly shepherd God's people. We should pray for our pastors and leaders to keep their wicks trimmed in prayer and Bible study, so their lights may burn brightly for the Lord. May all who are servants of the light serve our leaders as well so their sheep will trust in the Lord of light—Jesus!

"As long as it is day, we must do the works of him who sent me. Night is coming, when no one can work. While I am in the world, I am the light of the world" (John 9:4-5).

What area of darkness in my life needs the Lord's loving light? How can I be a light of love to point others to Jesus?

Related Readings
Psalm 4:6-8; John 12:36; Ephesians 5:8-14; 1 Thessalonians 5:5-11

Faith Overcomes

———— ◁∞▷ ————

To him who overcomes I will give to eat from the tree
of life, which is in the midst of the Paradise of God.

REVELATION 2:7 NKJV

Sometimes I question my faith. Is God really loving and just? If so, why is there so much injustice and hatred on the planet? Is my life really making a difference, or am I just another voice crying in the wilderness? Yet when I ask questions, the Holy Spirit gives me answers. He reminds me through Scripture what Christ has done, is doing, and will do. Trusting in Jesus means engaging your doubt with truth. Trust and truth resist giving up. As they move forward, faith eventually overcomes my doubts.

John reminds the churches that Christ has restored the Garden of Eden. Jesus's death and resurrection made a way beyond the flaming angel, who blocked the entrance into Paradise (Genesis 3:23-24). He replaced it with, "The one who believes in me will live" (John 11:25). The Tree of Life is accessible to those who embrace Christ as their life, and for them, heaven is top of mind. Our faith on earth overcomes because Jesus overcame life and death and made a way for eternal life. Trust in Jesus eventually wins, for He is already victorious.

———— ◁∞▷ ————

"This is the victory that has overcome the
world, even our faith" (1 John 5:4).

Are you overwhelmed by life? Do you feel stuck in a no-win situation? If so, have faith. The Lord has not brought you this far to abandon you. God has not given up on you, so don't give up on Him. Our experiences on earth are corrupted, but one day in heaven they will be incorruptible. We see glimpses of God's glory in the face of a cooing infant, in a cascading waterfall, and in the words of a forgiving friend. Look for God in life's small things and watch your faith grow.

Exercised faith is an overcoming faith. As a healthy body needs resistance and rest, so our faith grows stronger when stretched and challenged. Everyday life is an exercise of faith in Jesus. Will hard times harden or soften our hearts? Will good times grow our generosity or feed our greed? Our faith overcomes when we persevere in a job where we feel underpaid and underappreciated. Our faith overcomes when God's grace is sufficient for our painful circumstances. Our faith overcomes when we remain faithful to Jesus. Trust conquers this world as it anticipates the next.

"In this world you will have trouble. But take heart!
I have overcome the world" (John 16:33).

What life situation requires me to have an aggressive trust in the Lord?

Related Readings
John 15:18-21; Romans 8:37; 1 John 4:4; Revelation 2:26; 21:7

Immunity from Eternal Death

*Be faithful, even to the point of death, and I
will give you life as your victor's crown.*

REVELATION 2:10

My friend Regina went to be with the Lord. God did not heal her body, but He did release her soul to be with Him—forever. Cancer and death did not win, for once she breathed her last breath she awakened, victorious, in the presence of her Savior, Jesus Christ. For followers of Jesus, death is an immediate transition to be with Jesus. Regina greatly loved people. Faithful until her death, she was called home to worship Jesus in person!

Eternal death is forever separation from God—the Creator of life. Those who die without faith in Christ's death for sin's forgiveness and His resurrection for life eternal will find themselves banished from the Lord's presence. For believers in Jesus, eternal life is forever celebrated with Him. We better understand the love of God, having humbled ourselves in the fear of Him. There is a second death for those who die lost in their sins, but immunity for the saved—one death that transitions into eternal life.

"Now this is eternal life: that they know
you, the only true God, and Jesus Christ,
whom you have sent" (John 17:3).

Our faithfulness to the point of death is worthy of a victor's crown from Jesus. Any reward from Jesus is good. In humble worship and praise we place whatever rewards we receive at the feet of Jesus in honor of the One who won the victory for us. Faithfulness in this life is rewarded in the next. Just as an inheritance is given to those who can be trusted, so Christ gives an inheritance to those of His children He can trust with His rewards.

The quality of our conduct and character does not get us to heaven—faith in Christ does that. However, once we are in heaven, we will be rewarded according to our faithfulness on earth. Our humble service alongside our Savior in this life means we will humbly reign with Him in the next. Jesus prepares an eternal dwelling place for those who are prepared to be with Him. We shun sin now, preparing to live in a sinless society in eternity. We love all people now in preparation for loving and worshipping beside all people groups for eternity. Heaven is our immunity from hell.

⁓

"Then they will go away to eternal punishment, but
the righteous to eternal life" (Matthew 25:46).

Is my faith real and personal or only a facade—a cultural experience?

Related Readings
Psalm 16:11; Galatians 6:8; 1 John 5:11,13,20; Revelation 20:6,14; 21:8

11

Results of Faithfulness

—∞∞∞—

To the one who is victorious, I will give some of
the hidden manna. I will also give that person a
white stone with a new name written on it.

Faith in Jesus is our starting point with Him. As infant believers, we are totally dependent on adult believers to disciple us in the faith. We look to the more mature as models of faithful followers of Christ. We grow and mature, but not without drifting, doubting, and resisting along the way. We begin with faith in Jesus, we grow into faithfulness to Him, we enjoy the fruit of being with Jesus, and we are rewarded by Him. Our part is to remain faithful.

John wrote to the church in Pergamum, which struggled with unfaithfulness. Idolatry and sexual immorality infiltrated the local gathering of believers in Jesus. Sin infected the body of Christ, threatening its long-term health and stunting its short-term influence for God. Christ can change the culture, but this church shunned the Lord's Spirit and struggled to be "salt and light."

—∞∞∞—

"It gave me great joy when some believers came
and testified about your faithfulness to the truth,
telling how you continue to walk in it" (3 John 1:3).

The fruit of faithfulness is the manna (Exodus 16:33) of God's supernatural provision. Jesus satisfies our soul with heavenly manna—His

27

Word. As food and water sustain the human body, Scripture sustains the soul. Additionally, our heavenly Father renames us with a name in accordance with our identity in Christ. Cephas became Peter. He would be a rock of faith to build the church. James and John became the Sons of Thunder who boldly proclaimed the gospel. Your new name will be a commentary on your victorious life in the Lord.

Has faithfulness to Jesus become difficult for you? If so, take a step back and breathe in the fresh air of faith. Instead of praying only at a set time, let your life become *full* of prayer. The results of your faithfulness may not come to fruition immediately, but it's worth the wait. Your eternal rewards from Christ come when you go to be with Him. You won't grasp their significance until the day you possess and experience them. God rewards the faithful with His timeless love!

"Each of you should use whatever gift you have received to serve others, as faithful stewards of God's grace in its various forms" (1 Peter 4:10).

Where in my life do I need to remain faithful to Christ and His Word?

Related Readings
Proverbs 2:8; 2 Timothy 2:13; Hebrews 10:23; 11:11

Accelerated Development

———— ∞∞ ————

I know your deeds, your love and faith, your
service and perseverance, and that you are
now doing more than you did at first.

REVELATION 2:18-19

On vacation we like to ride bikes as a family. We take a leisurely ride on the sidewalk within view of the beach, or we enjoy the shade of live oaks that stand at attention like soldiers, Spanish moss draped over their limbs. The bikes operate smoothly as long as they move forward. But at a standstill they are wobbly at best—and totally useless when pedaling backward. Our life in Christ is similar. As long as we move forward in faith and love, we grow in grace. If we maintain a spiritual status quo, we fall or digress. Moving with God accelerates our growth in Him.

The church in Thyatira had digressed in their good deeds for Christ. They started out strong for the Lord, but their intolerance for sin devolved into tolerance for sexual immorality and idolatry. In an attempt to become relevant in the latest craze of the culture, the church became spiritually irrelevant. God blesses the surrounding culture through a church intolerant of what's wrong and tolerant of what's right. Is your church only remembered for its past glory days, or is it praised today for God's glory?

———— ∞∞ ————

"Forgetting what is behind and straining toward
what is ahead, I press on toward the goal to win

the prize for which God has called me heavenward
in Christ Jesus" (Philippians 3:13-14).

Does your faith reflect arrested or accelerated development? Did you start out strong and stay that way, or have you lost your spiritual momentum? Virtue must follow repentance of sin; otherwise, folly will soon fill the spiritual vacuum. Think of yourself as a vessel of Christ's service. Replace bad habits with intentional soul care and transformative heart disciplines.

Do more with the Lord—you will not be bored. Anyone can be average, so don't be just anyone. Be someone for God! A fully developed life in Christ is the most fulfilling life. More of Jesus means becoming more like Jesus—and doing more with Jesus. Accelerate your spiritual development.

"We ought always to thank God for you, brothers and
sisters, and rightly so, because your faith is growing
more and more, and the love all of you have for
one another is increasing" (2 Thessalonians 1:3).

How can I engage life with the Lord and accelerate the development of my faith?

Related Readings
1 Samuel 2:26; 1 Thessalonians 4:10; 1 Peter 2:2; Revelation 2:24

13

Access to Power

————❦————

*He who overcomes, and keeps My works until the
end, to him I will give power over the nations.*

REVELATION 2:26 NKJV

Several years ago a tornado ripped through the small town where I grew up. Everything in its path was uprooted and destroyed. For a period of time my in-laws were powerless—until we were able to find a generator and personally deliver it to their home. In a similar fashion, my life can be in disarray from sin's destruction. I feel powerless against forces outside my control, but God gives me access to His power. Grace is His generator, and it empowers my life during chaotic times.

John wrote to Christians who were dismissed and suppressed for their beliefs and their behavior. Humanly speaking, they were powerless in the face of an overreaching government and a hostile culture. However, the Holy Spirit, speaking through the pen of the apostle, reminded this influential minority—a band of believers in Christ— to remain faithful in their love for the Lord Jesus. The Holy Spirit's power supersedes society's criticism and apathy toward God. We diligently serve until the sunset of life, anticipating the morning star of our Savior's glory!

————❦————

"Peace I leave with you; my peace I give you. I do not
give to you as the world gives. Do not let your hearts
be troubled and do not be afraid" (John 14:27).

Do you feel powerless against a problem or a person? You may feel hopeless—even helpless—but your heavenly Father has the power to energize your faith in your fragile condition. The Spirit specializes in taking the weak and making them strong. An ailing condition qualifies you to be a recipient of God's grace. Satan tries to short-circuit your trust with his destructive lies, saying, "Your spouse doesn't really care. No one loves you." Or, "There are no solutions, and you will always be frustrated." But Jesus has answers. He says, "Remain in My love, and I will empower you with My wisdom."

Seek the Lord's wisdom in His Word. Truth is our flu shot against the virus of sickly thinking. Empowered by God's grace we are positioned to serve for the benefit of others. Our life on earth is a test in the faithful management of the Spirit's blessings, so we can be entrusted with more favor in eternity. The Lord's power, used for His glory, electrifies all of us who are citizens of the kingdom. The world will one day bow down to the One who gave away all power. So be bold, not shy, about accessing the gospel's power of God unto salvation!

———— ✺ ————

"The Spirit God gave us does not make us timid, but
gives us power, love and self-discipline" (2 Timothy 1:7).

Whom can I empower with my influence, support, and love?

Related Readings
Psalm 2:8; Isaiah 10:33; Romans 1:16; 1 Corinthians 1:18

Almost-Dead Church

*I know your deeds; you have a reputation
of being alive, but you are dead.*

REVELATION 3:1

Sadly, I have visited churches that once preached the gospel but are now closed, boarded up, and deserted. I have attended churches that are still open but spiritually anemic—only shells of cold religion with a handful of attendees. I have been to half-full churches in big, beautiful buildings. They are endowed with man's wealth—but not with heavenly riches. They are spiritually bankrupt. Thank God that many churches are still alive. Better to be a living church that disturbs the world than a dead church that is ignored by the world. Christ gives life to His bride, the church!

The church at Sardis was spiritually asleep. John's dramatic letter was a wake-up call. God's spokesman called out the local church for its conformity to the culture and society's mores. The Christian community as a whole—instead of being a vessel of transforming grace—had lost its influence on the world. Moral distinctiveness had eroded into moral relativity. The Sardis church once had a reputation for faithfulness but now was found faithless. Like a separated couple once admired for their model marriage, the church struggled with separation from God.

"This is why it is said: 'Wake up, sleeper, rise from the dead, and Christ will shine on you'" (Ephesians 5:14).

How can we, as sincere followers of Jesus, be a solution to a slumbering church? One way is to lead our church to pray. Before the workday begins, perhaps a few members can gather at the church to seek God. Ask Him for hearts to walk in humility, mercy, and justice. Intercede for the church's leaders to grow in their love for the Lord, their families, the faithful, and the lost. Pray all who name the name of Christ to experience an awakening of the Holy Spirit's fire.

The same fire of God that fell in answer to Elijah's prayers is the fire from heaven that will startle our souls to attention. The Holy Spirit's fire that immersed the masses at Pentecost and saved thousands is proof of the gospel's life-changing nature. The Spirit's influence burns brightest where Christians worship unashamedly, witness freely, and thoroughly repent of their sin. Like a comatose body that suddenly becomes conscious, our almost-dead churches will be revived when we as individual believers come alive. Ask Jesus to breathe His Spirit on His bride.

"Again Jesus said, 'Peace be with you! As the
Father has sent me, I am sending you.' And
with that he breathed on them and said,
'Receive the Holy Spirit'" (John 20:21-22).

How can I support the prayer effort at our church?

Related Readings
Isaiah 26:19; 60:1; Malachi 4:2; John 5:25; Romans 13:11;
1 Timothy 5:6

15

Walk in Humility

―――――∞∞∞―――――

They will walk with me, dressed in
white, for they are worthy.

REVELATION 3:4

The Christian life is a step-by-step walk of faith on the path of humility. The goal is not to get ahead of God with fleshly footsteps or to lag behind in fear. A walk with Jesus leads to a talk with Jesus through prayer. It is beautiful to know the Lord longs to linger in lockstep with the ones He loves.

We walk in humility because this is the cadence of Christ. Our heavenly Father does not want to see us sprinting through life without the Spirit's power. On the contrary, He smiles when He sees His servants waiting to accompany Him toward the next opportunity. A walk of humility takes the time to recognize surrounding relationships: the needs, wants, and dreams of others.

―――――∞∞∞―――――

"Now I, Nebuchadnezzar, praise, exalt and
honor the King of heaven, for all His works are
true and His ways just, and He is able to humble
those who walk in pride" (Daniel 4:37 NASB).

Are your steps pleasing to the Lord? Are you walking with or away from Jesus? Each step is important because it builds on a sequence of wisdom or foolishness. Each step of obedience reveals another footprint in God's will. You may not understand where the final step will take you, but you can be confident in the One who has directed it. Humility walks with the One who has already won and who reigns forever in heaven—Jesus!

—◦◦◦—

"Does he not see my ways and count
my every step?" (Job 31:4).

Humility grows amid the company of God and other believers. When you love others, you trust others. A proud person walks alone, but a community keeps you accountable and humble. Humility demands that we surrender our autonomy and voluntarily submit to wise counsel. Thus, when you walk with God, the light of His love exposes and disposes of the dark deeds of pride. As you walk in humility, grace sustains you!

—◦◦◦—

"Therefore I, the prisoner of the Lord, implore
you to walk in a manner worthy of the calling with
which you have been called, with all humility and
gentleness, with patience, showing tolerance for
one another in love" (Ephesians 4:1-2 NASB).

What ways is the Lord humbling my heart to walk in obedience with Him?

Related Readings
Proverbs 3:34; Isaiah 13:11; Micah 6:8; Matthew 23:12

Blotted Out of the Book of Life?

⎯⎯⎯⎯⎯ ∞ ⎯⎯⎯⎯⎯

*The one who is victorious will, like them, be
dressed in white. I will never blot out the name
of that person from the book of life.*

REVELATION 3:5

No, the redeemed of God cannot be blotted out of the book of life. Those who place their trust in Jesus for their salvation have their names permanently written in the Lord's book. In Christ alone, we are more than conquerors and victorious over sin, Satan, and death. Because we have conquered, our names are guaranteed; we cannot be erased from the book. We are secured by faith in Jesus, and our faithfulness is the fruit of being in the book of life.

The Lord says, "I will never leave you nor forsake you" (Hebrews 13:5 NKJV). With the same expression of love, the Lord says, "I will never blot out the name of that person from the book of life." Because of His unwavering character, God will never forsake or forget His faithful followers. There are some who say they are saved, but as life happens, their disingenuous faith leads them to stray from the flock of God. True followers return to the fold.

⎯⎯⎯⎯⎯ ∞ ⎯⎯⎯⎯⎯

"They went out from us, but they were not of
us; for if they had been of us, they would have
continued with us" (1 John 2:19 NKJV).

Has your name been written in the Lamb's book of life? If so, you can rest assured: Your heavenly Father's ink is permanent. Yes, your Lord and Savior's blood filled the inkwell of God's love so He could engrave your name on the pages of His profound grace and love. Pain will try to erase your name, but it won't. Doubt will try to remove your name, but it can't. Fear will seek to eliminate your eternal security, but it will fail. Your promise of everlasting life with the Lord is based on Jesus, not on your fleeting feelings. Faith can be certain of eternal security.

Have you left your community of Christ followers—even abandoned your faith? If so, be concerned that you are not one of the faithful. A wolf in sheep's clothing will one day be exposed by the judgment of God (Matthew 7:15). Embrace Christ, by faith, as the Son of the living God, who died on the cross for your sins and rose from death to give you life, forever to be with Him. Amen!

"All inhabitants of the earth will worship the beast—all whose names have not been written in the Lamb's book of life" (Revelation 13:8).

How can I express my gratitude to God for His assurance of salvation in Christ?

Related Readings
John 10:27-30; 1 Corinthians 12:6; Philippians 2:12-13; 1 John 5:13

Patient Endurance

―――――∞∞∞―――――

Since you have kept my command to endure
patiently, I will also keep you from the hour of trial.
REVELATION 3:10

My high school studies were not my best effort. Many times I would wait until the last minute and spend late nights memorizing information. Yes, I could repeat a lot of facts, but I comprehended very little. My college undergraduate and graduate days were much different. Rita and I married after our freshman year, and as a husband, I felt responsible for excelling in my education. Some professors rewarded those who patiently worked hard, who took to heart the lectures and completed the homework exercises. The disciplined learners were exempt from the final exam.

Christ commended the church at Philadelphia for keeping His commands and for their patient endurance. Yes, only one of the seven Asian churches rose above the world's expectations; they imperfectly but wholeheartedly followed Jesus. This local body of believers hid God's word in their hearts so they would not be ashamed and feel the need to hide from their compassionate Creator. Their persistence in patiently following the Lord strengthened their endurance. God provides a way out of temptation, and He offers grace to carry us through trials. He commends perseverance.

―――――∞∞∞―――――

"You need to persevere so that when you

have done the will of God, you will receive
what he has promised" (Hebrews 10:36).

Is your church branded by the community as a place that loves the Lord? Does your church clearly express its love for people? Evidence of love may include sharing the gospel of Jesus Christ with passion and compassion, sleeping at the bedside of someone struggling to survive an illness, caring for a foster child who yearns for a parent with capacity to care, clothing the homeless, or feeding the hungry. A loving church looks for ways to meet human needs in the name of Jesus.

Those who endure in the faith make it a priority to know, understand, and obey the commands of Christ. Quiet perseverance is a mark of the Master. A disciple full of the Spirit provides a safe place for those whose hearts hurt. In their presence you feel no need to parse your words—only to say your piece and trust the kind listener to lovingly remove the chaff from the wheat. Christ commends patient kindness that endures hard dialogue. Those who persevere in faith are exempt from eternal punishment.

"If this is so, then the Lord knows how to rescue the
godly from trials and to hold the unrighteous for
punishment on the day of judgment" (2 Peter 2:9).

Where can I serve in my church? How can I quietly and kindly love others?

Related Readings
Psalm 37:33; Matthew 24:14; 1 John 3:23; Revelation 6:10

18

Keep Faith in Jesus

⸺∞∞⸺

*I am coming quickly. Hold tight what you
have, so that no one will take your crown
[by leading you to renounce the faith].*

REVELATION 3:11 AMP

I'm a former 10K runner and a one-time half marathoner (13.1 miles). I trained for the longer race with a friend. We enjoyed the camaraderie and provided needed accountability for each other. The preparation for the half marathon was hard but fulfilling. On race day we were in our best shape. The weather, though a chilly 35 degrees, was sunny with a brilliant blue sky. There was only one problem: I was very sick with the flu. The first ten miles went fast. The last three miles were as slow as molasses, but my friend waited and helped me finish well.

Jesus reminds the church and individual believers to keep their faith in Him. Christ instructed His followers to hold on to the hope of His return, not allowing individual naysayers or the cynical culture to cause them to renounce their reliance on God. The race of faith requires preparation, perseverance, and faithful friends who can help us finish well. The victor's crown is not royalty, but a wreath of righteousness given by the Righteous One—Jesus. Yes, when we faithfully hang on to Jesus, we experience the anticipation of His eternal joy!

⸺∞∞⸺

"Though now you do not see Him, yet believing,
you rejoice with joy inexpressible and full of

> glory, receiving the end of your faith—the
> salvation of your souls" (1 Peter 1:8-9 NKJV).

We know in our heads that God's peace protects us from anxious thoughts, but only when we take this to heart do we live by faith and not in fear. We also know that God is sovereign, so since the Lord is in control, do we as followers of Jesus really need to emotionally hyperventilate over the world's chaotic condition? Some Christians seem no different from non-Christians in their fearful predictions of depression and despair. Faith hopes in God.

Rather than gutting it out with God on your own, remember that Christians are better together. As we run our race of faith, some will stumble and need one or several of us to help them up. Perhaps we will need to mend them before they step back onto the track. If weary, we must stop, rest, and hydrate our souls. Those who run the race of faith together have a higher probability of finishing well. Keep your faith in Jesus strong by looking forward to the crown.

———∞∞∞———

> "The Lord, the righteous Judge, will award to me on
> that day—and not only to me, but also to all who
> have longed for his appearing" (2 Timothy 4:8).

Who would benefit from my help and encouragement?

Related Readings
1 Corinthians 9:25; 1 Thessalonians 2:19; 1 Peter 1:13;
Revelation 2:10

19

Stability and Security

———⚬⚬⚬———

The one who is victorious I will make a pillar in the temple of my God. Never again will they leave it. I will write on them the name of my God.

REVELATION 3:12

Uncertainty is a certainty of life. Economic uncertainty. Political uncertainty. Financial uncertainty. Relational uncertainty. Physical uncertainty. Those who focus on life's uncertainties are certain to be preoccupied by fear and anxiety. Being consumed by uncertainty is like traveling on extremely winding roads while sitting in the backseat of a car; you begin to feel the nausea of emotional motion sickness. Has uncertainty caused fear to overcome your faith?

The Lord describes an eternal environment of stability and security—a place with no fear because all of the citizens of God's city are redeemed by Jesus the Lamb. The city of God is governed by King Jesus, who keeps all His promises. His promises of no more sin, sorrow, or suffering are secure. His guarantee of our resurrection and reigning with Him stabilizes our soul. We are rock-solid pillars of faith who worship the Lord in His temple. Emotional stability and spiritual security accompany those who travel with Jesus.

———⚬⚬⚬———

"The fruit of that righteousness will be peace; its effect will be quietness and confidence forever" (Isaiah 32:17).

Perhaps a relationship has your stomach in knots. Uncertainty, foolish choices, and selfish motivations may have overcome what started out as a safe and secure union. Difficult conversations can lead to conflict and confusion. When these things happen, seek your heavenly Father for humility. He can help your heart to grow in grace and wisdom. Be honest with a mentor or trained counselor who can coach you through this emotional "pain cycle" and into a "peace cycle." Learn skills like effective confession and repentance to create ongoing forgiveness and healing.

Look to the Lord's assurance of what He has for you now and throughout eternity. Life on earth offers little hope or help, so build a foundation of trust in your heavenly Father. Move out of the backseat of unbelief (marked by emotional motion sickness) and sit up front in the passenger seat of trust with Christ as your chauffeur. Though sometimes dim and misty, the eyes of faith see your final destination—and it is good because God is good. Submit daily to the Holy Spirit's cleansing and filling. He infuses a soul with stability and security. There's victory in Jesus.

—∞—

"Thanks be to God! He gives us the victory through
our Lord Jesus Christ" (1 Corinthians 15:57).

Whom can I seek for wise counsel to deal with relational conflict?

Related Readings
Job 11:18; 2 Timothy 1:10; Hebrews 2:14; 1 John 4:4; 5:4;
Revelation 21:7

Cultural Christianity

*I know your deeds, that you are neither cold nor
hot. I wish you were either one or the other!*

REVELATION 3:15

Cultural Christianity has a form of godliness but no faith in Christ. There is a resemblance to righteousness, but not an authentic heart change. Because the culture may understand the tenets of Christianity, a citizen may think their birthright into that society makes them a Christian. However, understanding without conversion is just head knowledge. Familiarity does breed contempt when cultural Christianity replaces personal faith with a general feel-good faith.

Jesus describes the convenience of being lukewarm. If it's convenient, I'll say I am a Christian; if it's not convenient, I'll act as if I'm not a Christian. This is the motto of men and women who use Christianity to further self-interest. Joy is the reaction of those who first hear about Jesus, but when their emotional foundation is tested, they fall away— faithless. They may say the right words, even attend church, but their heart is far from God. A convenient Christian is a counterfeit who lacks true belief and conviction.

"Those on the rocky ground are the ones who
receive the word with joy when they hear it, but
they have no root. They believe for a while, but in
the time of testing they fall away" (Luke 8:13).

Have you been genuinely converted to Christ? Have you humbled your heart like a little child and embraced Jesus Christ as the resurrected Lord and Savior of your life? Your individual conversion to Christ is a significant source of strength for your church, community, and family. You become salt and light for a society in search of its soul. Preachers, lawyers, judges, students, mechanics, coaches, teachers, homemakers, executives, artists, and athletes who love Jesus begin to influence friends for Jesus. Converted Christians change the culture for Christ.

Cultural Christians blend into the culture. Converted Christians influence the culture. The apron strings of your parents' faith cannot make you right with Almighty God. Your beliefs cannot be a barnacle on the cruise ship of someone else's conversion. Personal conversion is your only qualifier for heaven after death and abundant life on earth. Cultural Christians are only an imitation of real intimacy and salvation in Jesus. Repent, therefore, and be converted to Christ.

―∞∞∞―

"Repent therefore and be converted, that your sins
may be blotted out, so that times of refreshing may
come from the presence of the Lord" (Acts 3:19 NKJV).

Do I need to escape the comfort of cultural Christianity?
Have I accepted the transforming power of being an authentic convert of Christ?

Related Readings
Psalm 51:13; Acts 9:1-6; 15:3; 2 Corinthians 5:13-14;
1 Timothy 3:6

21

Repulsive to the Lord

—⊶⊷⊶—

*Because you are lukewarm—neither hot nor
cold—I am about to spit you out of my mouth.*

REVELATION 3:16

Institutions of God can lose their intimacy with God. Like the marble floor of a stoic cathedral, the culture of a once vibrant ministry can become cold and hard. Indeed, Christ calls out His church to make a clear commitment to His commands and not waffle like a reluctant bride or groom at the altar. A community of faith can fossilize when it isn't faithful to the tenets of the truth.

Lukewarm disciples are repulsive to the Lord.

Is your faith on fire, or is it simmering under the influence of sin? There is no room for neutrality toward religion rooted in Christ. Are you for Him or against Him? Apathy is a vote against Him. Passivity to prayer and public worship is lukewarm leadership for your home. Thus, use the beginning of the New Year to attend church with your family. Join a friend in a yearlong Bible reading plan, or sign up for a mission to serve the poor.

—⊶⊷⊶—

"This is war, and there is no neutral ground. If you're
not on my side, you're the enemy; if you're not helping,
you're making things worse" (Luke 11:23 MSG).

We may want to make everyone happy, but how can we at the expense of disappointing our heavenly Father? We should be wary

47

of companions who cool our commitment to Christ. Our red-hot hearts of righteousness ought to rub off on those unsure of their salvation. Our humility and compassionate care should be like kerosene to another's flickering flame of faith. Our combustible love explodes another's faith in God.

Therefore, come out of the closet with your commitment to Christ. Do not be ashamed of the gospel, but instead proclaim it. Because you have been given so much, you can give much! Be bold in your faith without being obnoxious. The cross of Christ carries its own offense. Look to your heavenly Father to fuel your faith and to the Holy Spirit to ignite it. Burn hot and bright for God's Son Jesus Christ!

—∞∞—

"Elijah went before the people and said, 'How long will you waver between two opinions? If the LORD is God, follow him; but if Baal is God, follow him'" (1 Kings 18:21).

What passion of mine can the Spirit enflame in my heart to mirror God's passions?

Related Readings

Joshua 24:15; Psalm 119:113; Matthew 6:24; Romans 12:11

22

The Best Advice

I counsel you to buy from me gold refined in the fire,
so you can become rich; and white clothes to wear.

REVELATION 3:18

The advice of well-meaning people is not always best. They advise us when to buy or sell, give or lend, spend or save. In the case of a relationship, they suggest when we should give it a second chance or when we should break it off. When we consider changing jobs, they opine about whether we should stay with a job or change. Sincere counsel that sounds right may not be the best advice. Only Christ gives counsel that is accurate 100 percent of the time.

In Revelation, Jesus's very insightful counsel exposes the church's inability to see its unhealthy condition. His remedy is the application of His Spirit's salve to reveal their need for righteousness. Those who recognize their needy state are in a position to receive counsel, but those stuck in denial live perpetually in pain. Eventually severe dysfunction drives people and organizations to recognize their sickly condition, but the longer the delay, the harder it is to fully recover. Only spiritual health can truly satisfy!

"So if you have not been trustworthy in
handling worldly wealth, who will trust
you with true riches?" (Luke 16:11).

Wealth of heart is what our heavenly Father desires most for us. Abundance is the asset our generous God offers to His children— abundance of joy, relationships, and all we need to live a fulfilling life. Yet the riches of Christ are not without cost. As our faith is tried by the fires of adversity and success, we must remain faithful. To remain faithful we must heed the best advice, which comes from our Creator's wisdom.

Are you open to advice? Have you truly humbled yourself to admit you are in need of help from God and others? The closer a person is to an issue, the harder it is for them to see the best solution. Faith takes a step back and invites in a third party to help parse the problem. The best counsel comes from Christ. What does He think about your situation? How does Jesus want to love you amid your pain? Listen to the Lord. Look around to see Him at work and receive His best advice.

"First seek the counsel of the LORD" (1 Kings 22:5).

Who has experience and wisdom to offer me? To whom may I turn for wise counsel?

Related Readings
Job 12:13; Psalms 16:7; 32:8; 119:24; Proverbs 16:1-9; Romans 11:33-35

23

Love Initiates Intimacy

*Here I am! I stand at the door and knock. If anyone
hears my voice and opens the door, I will come
in and eat with that person, and they with me.*

REVELATION 3:20

Years ago, my friend Gale called with a passion to pray for me. How refreshing! As a vocational minister of the gospel, I was normally the one offering prayers, but not this time. For a full year Gale called me every Friday. He asked for an update on my prior week's prayer and any new needs I had, and then he led us in prayer together. Wow, this man loved me in the most intimate, helpful way! I gained inner strength by his love, and his prayers initiated intimacy.

Jesus vividly paints the picture of Himself standing at the door. The Lord is the gentle guest waiting outside, ready to come in and engage the occupant. He is generous company, and He receives and gives hospitality. His holy presence offers prayers on behalf of all those in need of His grace. His sacrificial life, death, and resurrection introduce the gift of salvation to everyone who invites Him in and trusts Him wholeheartedly. Jesus initiates intimacy with those who need Him as Savior and with those who desire a relationship with Him as friend.

*"It will be good for those servants whose
master finds them watching when he
comes...He will dress himself to serve...and
will come and wait on them" (Luke 12:37).*

Have you received the loving intimacy initiated by the Lord Jesus Christ? Have you received Him into your life as your personal Savior? If not, simply pray, "Jesus, I trust You for the forgiveness of my sins. I believe You died on the cross and rose from the grave. You are my God." Perhaps Jesus is already in your life, but you need a fresh infusion of His intimate love. Just as opening the shutters invites in warmth, so opening one's heart to Christ's love invites in warm intimacy.

Who needs to share intimacy with you? A spouse, child, parent, sibling, or friend? You can't control their response, but you can initiate unhurried time together. Make it easier to meet by planning ahead for both of you. Budget time and money. Intimacy is not easily achieved, but the fruits of trust, joy, and knowledge are worth the effort. Love initiates intimacy!

―――⊶∞⊷―――

"God is love. Whoever lives in love lives in God, and God in them" (1 John 4:16).

Who needs my persistent love, so we can really grow to know each other deeply?

Related Readings
Proverbs 8:17; Zephaniah 3:17; Romans 8:10; James 5:9; 1 John 4:8-9

Fight the Good Fight

───※───

*To the one who is victorious, I will give the
right to sit with me on my throne.*

REVELATION 3:21

Soldiers are my heroes—those who fight for freedom and ensure domestic tranquility. Some are newly enlisted on their way to boot camp, a few are enrolled in officer training, and others provide technical support or manage administrative details. Then there are the fighters on the battlefront—daily putting their lives on the line. Some live and some die, but all sacrifice. War is ugly, messy, and hellish in its fierce engagements, but battles can be won with unity and God's favor.

John describes a scene in heaven where the final battle has been fought, weapons cease to exist, weary bodies are in repose, minds are not churning with activity, and emotions are at ease. Because Jesus fought the good fight while He lived on earth, He now reigns with His Father in heaven. Christ overcame the devil's temptations so that we might overcome as well. He conquered evil with good so we can conquer too. He endured suffering that we might endure with Him. Jesus lived, died, and came to life—so we can live, die, and come to life!

───※───

"Fight the good fight of the faith" (1 Timothy 6:12).

Do you have a relationship battlefront to reengage? You may need to fight for your marriage, a child, a parent, or a friend. Relational passivity is not an option because love initiates. Learn to fight fair for the one you love—but fight! Quiet resentment is as bad or worse than screeching demands. Do not shock others like an emotional stealth bomber, or blow them away with a verbal machine gun. Instead, fight for their affection by serving and loving them in ways that make them feel valued. You fight a good fight when you assume the best and forgive.

How do you know if you are engaged in fighting the good fight with God? Prayer is the weapon your enemy fears the most. Prayer can go places you may be unable to go: school, political arenas, business trips, mission fields, hospitals, retirement homes, and hearts. Prayer aligns your heart with the Lord's heart of love and humility. Love gives strength from above, and humility gives unlimited access to His grace. Fight with God's weapons, not with the world's defeated arsenal. With Jesus, you reign!

"The Lord will fight for you; you need
only to be still" (Exodus 14:14).

Whom do I need to love right where they are and trust God to lead them where they need to be?

Related Readings

Numbers 32:27; 1 Samuel 25:28; John 18:36; Acts 5:39; 2 Timothy 4:7

25

Listen for God's Voice

*The voice I had first heard speaking to me
like a trumpet said, "Come up here, and I will
show you what must take place after this."*

REVELATION 4:1

God's voice has not vanished. He has not lost His voice because of overuse. His vocal cords are not strained but strong. God does not cough or become congested. His voice is clear and intelligible. His voice is all around us; listen and be in awe. Thunder and lightning display His glory in the heavens. We hear His thunder and gaze up in both fear and amazement. His voice reminds us of His glory. The Lord's majestic presence thunders from above.

John wrote earlier about Jesus standing at the door, waiting to be invited in. Now the Lord opens the door to heaven and invites John to come in and experience Him. The voice of God sounds like a trumpet, similar to the sound of a trumpet announcing the resurrection of the dead in Christ (1 Thessalonians 4:16). The Lord is drawing John closer to His throne of grace and worship, so He might reveal to His humble servant His vision of things to come. Worship and grace escort us into the presence of our heavenly Father, who is ready to show us His ways.

"God's voice thunders in marvelous ways; he does great things beyond our understanding" (Job 37:5).

God's voice can be powerful when applied in our lives. He can be stern in discipline or tender in grace. The powerful voice of Jesus called Lazarus back from the dead, and on the cross He interceded to His heavenly Father for forgiveness on behalf of His enemies. Use your voice to pray for people who are dead in their sin and in need of a Savior. Lift up your voice on behalf of others who have offended or hurt you. God hears your voice.

God's voice is majestic and regal. He is enthroned above all His creation. Jesus is our King of kings and Lord of lords. When He speaks, we listen. His words matter most. The Bible is the wisdom of His words in written form. His voice speaks through the pages of Scripture, so pay attention to what He tells you and obediently apply it to your life. Tell others what Christ tells you. Those of us who hear the voice of God cannot keep quiet, so be a clean conduit for His voice to speak.

"The LORD confides in those who fear him; he makes his covenant known to them" (Psalm 25:14).

What is the Spirit saying to my soul? How can I distinguish God's voice from competing voices?

Related Readings
Psalm 18:13; Jeremiah 6:10; Philippians 1:14; 1 Thessalonians 4:16

26

Holy, Holy, Holy

Day and night they never stop saying "'Holy, holy, holy is the Lord God Almighty,' who was, and is, and is to come."
REVELATION 4:8

The holiness of our heavenly Father cannot be completely comprehended by the human mind. His purity burns so brightly, the dross of our sinful deeds melts in the presence of His pure character. Just as Moses took cover in the cleft of the rock as God passed by, so we take shelter in the refuge of our Savior Jesus to be able to handle the glory of our great God. His name is above all names—not to be spoken in vain, but evoked in humble adoration.

John describes a 24/7 majestic worship experience. Similar to Isaiah's famous vision of reverent angelic beings adoring God (Isaiah 6:1-5), each person of the Trinity is praised as absolutely holy and worthy of all glory and honor. The Lord God Almighty who was, and is, and is to come is 100 percent perfection in His pure love and affection! We seek Him alone in worship, for no other is worthy of our radical devotion. Our worship resonates forever.

"Holy, holy, holy is the LORD Almighty; the
whole earth is full of his glory" (Isaiah 6:3).

Our heavenly Father's holiness is the standard of sinless perfection. Though we will never achieve perfection in this life, His Holy Spirit continues to perfect our faith and character to make us more like

Christ. As children of the Holy One, we are set apart to be holy as He is holy. However, be careful not to fall into the "holier than thou" trap. Sin is never comfortable in the presence of purity. We are only channels for the Spirit to convict the hearts of those we love on behalf of Jesus. We pray for His holiness to shine through us.

We are friends with Jesus and we partner with the Holy Spirit, but we are submissive children of our Father, the Most High—our great and glorious God. We bow now in individual preparation for the day after our death, when we will pray with all in glorious acclamation. Can you see His holy aura in your reverent worship of your heavenly Father? Esteem His holy name!

—⚬⚬⚬—

"At the name of Jesus every knee should bow, in heaven and on earth and under the earth, and every tongue acknowledge that Jesus Christ is Lord" (Philippians 2:10-11).

What songs of praise cause me to lift my heart in adoration of God's holiness?

Related Readings
Isaiah 52:13; Daniel 7:14; Acts 2:33; 1 Peter 1:15-16

27

Heartfelt Worship

⌒∞∞⌒

*The twenty-four elders fall down before him who sits on
the throne and worship him who lives for ever and ever.*

REVELATION 4:10

I could see love in their faces. Some leathery and wrinkled from the
toils and trials of life, others youthful, smooth cheeked, and white
toothed—all beaming with the joy of Jesus. My fifth trip in ten years
to India felt like my first. Why? I'm not sure, but something about the
heart of the people refreshed me: pure and full of faith. Their Hindi
prayers and praise escorted my soul into the presence of our Savior. The
Holy Spirit, like a knife through hot butter, cut to the depths of my
being. I wept in the presence of great lovers of God.

In this verse, the 24 elders represent the church and all believers
who lift their heartfelt worship to the Lord God Almighty. All followers
of Jesus will be rewarded at the judgment seat of God (Romans 14:10).
As the righteous cast crowns before the throne of God, they are only
offering back what is rightfully God's in humble adoration and honor.
Heartfelt worship keeps the glory of God at the center of attention—
not the works of man.

⌒∞∞⌒

"My heart rejoices in the LORD; in the LORD
my horn is lifted high…There is no one
holy like the LORD" (1 Samuel 2:1-2).

Magnify the Lord in worship; rejoice and praise His holy name in song. God has done extraordinary things for you, in you, and through you. He created you in His image, and He saved you to grow into the image of His Son Jesus. As you fear and adore Him, He pours out His abundant grace and mercy on you. Your praise models gratitude to God, empowering the next generation to rejoice mightily in Jesus Christ!

Like the mighty Mississippi River, thankfulness overflows the soul that sings out to its Savior. As we adore the Lord for His loving presence, He awards us with security. We worship the Holy One in the rarified air of His righteousness, while His Spirit bestows holiness into our hearts. Our heartfelt praise guarantees engagement with God. The Holy Spirit's influence is without borders. Like John, we are instruments of Christ's work in and through us.

"I will perpetuate your memory through all
generations; therefore the nations will praise
you for ever and ever" (Psalm 45:17).

Who in the next generation needs me to model adoration of God?

Related Readings
Psalm 78:4; Isaiah 61:10; 1 Timothy 4:10; 1 Peter 2:10-12

28

Intelligent Design

You are worthy, our Lord and God, to receive glory
and honor and power, for you created all things, and
by your will they were created and have their being.

REVELATION 4:10-11

God is the intelligence behind the design of creation and life. He is the architect of the universe and the engineer of eternal life. He is the wisdom behind the world. The soft, pinkish-blue sunset, He designed. The brilliant, bold, and bright sunrise cascading over the treetops, He designed. The pure snowcapped mountains projecting toward heaven in reverence, He designed. The gorgeous and luscious green vegetation, He designed.

The deep-blue seas and the baby-blue sky, He designed. The furry and ferocious animals, He designed. The multicolored bugs and beetles, He designed. The chirping sparrows, the clacking seagulls, and the hovering hummingbirds, He designed. Fish, shrimp, whales, and penguins, He designed. Most fascinating, the intricate design of water and flesh called the human body, He designed.

"In the beginning God created the heavens
and the earth" (Genesis 1:1).

He is the intelligent designer of earth and mankind. It takes more arrogance than faith to believe otherwise. He gave us intelligence to recognize that He is the intelligent designer. If we cannot accept that

God is behind the design, then we are not being intellectually honest. The evidence is overwhelming. Its affirmation quietly rests within our hearts. Its confirmation floods our minds, and its declaration explodes from our mouths.

Anything good that has been accomplished by God through you will be laid at the feet of Jesus. Your crown of rewards will not be proudly worn on your head; rather, it will be placed before the throne of God. Heaven is all about Him. Just like Christmas is all about Christ, our time on earth is all about our preparation for Him in heaven.

Worshipping Him on earth is but an appetizing morsel of what we will have to feast on in glory. His design of you and creation is not only intelligent; it is also good. Therefore, worship Him now in preparation of worshipping Him later. All praise, honor, power, and glory go to God! He desires it, and He deserves it. His intelligent design reflects His majesty.

"Put on the new self, created to be like God in true righteousness and holiness" (Ephesians 4:24).

Do I have an intelligent understanding of God's intelligent design? How can I grow my understanding of my Creator so I can creatively communicate it to His creation?

Related Readings
Psalms 22:27-31; 36:6-7; Romans 1:18-23; 2 Peter 3:8

29

Scripture's Timeless Truth

———⚬≈⚬———

*Then I saw in the right hand of him who sat on
the throne a scroll with writing on both sides and
sealed with seven seals. And I saw a mighty angel
proclaiming in a loud voice, "Who is worthy
to break the seals and open the scroll?"*

REVELATION 5:1-2

We are blessed when we seek counsel from the wise, but when we receive direction from Almighty God in His Word, we can rest assured. The Bible is the baseline for our beliefs and behavior—the first and the final say for faith-based living. A day without scriptural intake is like missing three meals. God's Word nourishes the soul, is a trailblazer for truth, and leads us into His very best for our lives.

As He sits enthroned, He holds the scroll of Scripture in His right hand—His Word in general and this Revelation prophecy in particular. The Lord's precious words are sealed seven times and are kept in safekeeping, awaiting the worthy Lamb of God to open them. The counsel of God will be revealed and the mystery of His love and judgment clarified by Christ. Even today the Holy Spirit is our guide into all truth so that we may confidently follow Jesus.

———⚬≈⚬———

*"Consult God's instruction and the testimony of
warning. If anyone does not speak according to this
word, they have no light of dawn" (Isaiah 8:20).*

You endure as you learn and apply the enduring Word of the Lord to your life. Have you encountered a roadblock in parenting? If so, Scripture has insight into seeing exactly how to love your child at their point of need. Are you experiencing an unreasonable individual at work or in your family? The Bible gives instructions on how to unselfishly serve those who are full of themselves. Come to Christ and listen to His voice as He speaks to you through His Word.

A word from the Lord gives hope in the face of discouragement, wisdom for understanding, and courage to confront injustice. Scriptures planted in the human heart are seeds of faith for the soul. If you hide the life-giving Word of God in a humbled heart, you will be able to give life to others. What does God think? This is the first question for followers of Jesus Christ; and fortunately for His children, His Holy Spirit brings to life the pages of His Word in prayer. Study to know the truth and listen to apply it. Scripture gives stamina to your faith.

"He replied, 'My mother and brothers are those who hear God's word and put it into practice'" (Luke 8:21).

What area of my life needs instruction and encouragement from God's Word?

Related Readings
Genesis 15:1; 1 Samuel 3:1-7; 2 Timothy 2:9; Hebrews 1:3

30

How to Deal with Disappointment

*I wept and wept because no one was found who
was worthy to open the scroll or look inside.*

REVELATION 5:4

Everyone deals with disappointment—some more than others. These letdowns vary in scope: another year of no raises at work, a friend's forgetfulness, a lost opportunity, a teenager's poor choices, a missed deadline, a relative's financial woes, a boss's oversight, an injured body, or unexpected medical issues. In this world troubles abound, but in Christ, peace is profound.

John wept over the inaccessibility of God's Word. In his vision of coming events in heaven, the apostle experienced the disappointment of needing someone worthy of unleashing the scroll of Scripture. But immediately a wise elder reassured the prophet that the Lion of the tribe of Judah—Jesus Christ—is worthy to unleash the truth. In unison an explosion of worship echoed throughout heaven: "Worthy is the Lamb!" In Christ we are worthy to access His Word.

"God may make you worthy of his calling, and
that by his power he may bring to fruition your
every desire for goodness and your every deed
prompted by faith" (2 Thessalonians 1:11).

Disappointment can lead to disobedience. The hole in our heart is meant to grow our dependency on God because He brings wholeness and holiness to a lacerated soul. The Lord heals hurt feelings when we offer forgiveness, but disappointment feeds selfishness when we don't get our way. So be wise. If your frustration overwhelms your faith, you can lose patience and respect. Allow your trust in Jesus to trump testy relationships. Adjust your expectations to His standard.

Appointments with God help us to deal with disappointment. He gives us rest when we are restless. He gives us calm when there is calamity. He gives us peace when there is chaos. He gives us trust when there is distrust. But how do we respond to those who disappoint us? We see them as our heavenly Father sees them—sheep in need of a shepherd. Friends falter, so will we judge them from a distance or love them up close?

Let God's love cover your disappointment like a warm blanket. By faith, accept a friend's forgiveness and your Savior's acceptance.

———— ❧ ————

"Then you will know that I am the Lord; those who
hope in me will not be disappointed" (Isaiah 49:23).

How can I grow my love and obedience to God?

Related Readings
Job 6:20; Psalms 5:3; 22:5; John 6:60-71; 2 Corinthians 8:5;
James 1:6-8

31

Holy Spirit Unleashed

⧓

*The Lamb had seven horns and seven eyes, which are
the seven spirits of God sent out into all the earth.*

REVELATION 5:6

The Holy Spirit assumes a variety of roles in support of those surrendered to their Savior. They include the Spirit of wisdom and
revelation to know Christ better, the Spirit of truth to guide in all truth,
the Spirit of holiness to live in the power of the resurrected life of Christ,
the Spirit of self-control to resist temptations and to remain resilient
through trials, and the Spirit of love to receive strength and security.
One Spirit distributes many gifts to Christ's followers.

Jesus, the Lamb of God, was the final sacrifice for sin, and that sacrifice unleashed the power of the Holy Spirit at Pentecost. The cross was
a catalyst for the Spirit's manifest power throughout the ages. The seven
horns represent perfect power, and the seven eyes express the explosion
of the Spirit throughout the world as prophesied by Zechariah. What
the apostle John envisions is a global outpouring of the Holy Spirit to
draw the lost into the light of salvation, to heal the brokenhearted, and
to gather the church to worship in the Spirit's power. The Holy Spirit
is unleashed to empower!

⧓

"I will pour out my Spirit on all people" (Joel 2:28).

Does your heart communicate fluently with the Holy Spirit, or
does He sound foreign to you? God's teacher—His Spirit—interprets

His language of love. Through the power of the Spirit you are able to adore your Lord and experience focused worship. Yes, His sweet Spirit lifts your soul toward your loving heavenly Father. And the Holy Spirit not only facilitates faithful worship but also leads you in God's will. The Holy Spirit partners with the heart to fuel a life of radical love and obedience. The Spirit discerns.

The Holy Spirit delivers the gospel message with compelling conviction, drawing humans toward heaven. The Spirit is the spark that lights the fuse of the good news. Evangelism energized by the Spirit will not be stopped by persecution, pride, or indifference. The Holy Spirit heals broken hearts, births joy out of sadness, and offers hope amid awful conditions. The Spirit is unleashed to set captives free!

———— ∞ ————

"The Spirit of the Lord is on me, because
he has anointed me to proclaim good
news to the poor" (Luke 4:18).

Consider a 24-hour silent retreat to recalibrate your heart with the Holy Spirit.

Related Readings
Isaiah 61:1-3; Romans 8:2; 1 Corinthians 2:12; 12:13;
2 Corinthians 3:17

32

Purpose of Praise

*To him who sits on the throne and to the Lamb be praise
and honor and glory and power, for ever and ever.*

REVELATION 5:13

We tend to think less of those who want us to think more of them. People who demand praise or require affirmation for every little action are emotionally unfit. An enlarged ego has to be told how much it is esteemed, but a small ego esteems others better than itself (Romans 12:10). Yet, the Lord Almighty expects us to praise Him. Why? He is all-sufficient, but God knows we are needy. Praising Him changes our perspectives and motivates us to pray.

The Lamb (Jesus) accompanies God the Father, who sits on His heavenly throne, surrounded by His Spirit (Revelation 1:4). This heavenly expression of the triune God compels Christ followers to exclaim, "Praise, honor, glory, and power forever and ever!" Our home in heaven is a worship fest of God the Father, God the Son, and God the Spirit. Just mentioning the name "Jesus" stirs our souls to thanksgiving and wholehearted devotion. Praise points us to the Lamb who was slain for our salvation. Praise expresses gratitude.

"John saw Jesus coming toward him and
said, 'Look, the Lamb of God, who takes
away the sin of the world!'" (John 1:29).

Moreover, praising Jesus is our opportunity to tell people about Jesus. Just as we say, "You have to see this movie," or, "This book will challenge your thinking and make you a better person"—thus we praise God so others might experience Him. It's okay to say, "I still have issues, but since I trusted Jesus as my Savior, I have forgiveness, peace, and purpose." We release our inner praise with outer thanksgiving to the Lord. Praise consummates our full appreciation of Christ.

What is the purpose of praise? It gives soul alignment to those saved by the grace of God. It offers to our Lord and Savior what He deserves and desires (not what He needs). The Lord knows our praise of Him is what's best for us. Praise Him for His majestic creation, for He is the Creator. Praise Him for His precious children, for He is their heavenly Father. Praise Him for His good gifts, for He is a generous Giver. Praise His holy name!

"Sing the praises of the LORD, you his faithful
people; praise his holy name" (Psalm 30:4).

How can my praise of God influence others to praise God?

Related Readings
Psalms 103:1; 146:1-2; Malachi 2:2; Luke 10:21; Romans 11:36; 1 Peter 2:9

33

Trial by Fire

—❧—

I looked, and there before me was a white horse!
Its rider held a bow, and he was given a crown, and
he rode out as a conqueror bent on conquest.

REVELATION 6:2

A trial by fire purifies. We normally do not invite trials or look forward to them as tools God uses for our purification, but they compel us toward intimacy and dependence on our heavenly Father. Satan's desire is to drive us from God during our adversity, but God's heart is to draw us unto Him as life heats up. Indeed, fiery trials seem to never let up or give up. The refining fires of heaven burn away pride and replace it with humility. Fear evaporates and is overcome by trust. God removes anxiety and replaces it with His peace. Refining fire is hot, but you are not alone.

The tribulation is a time when all hell breaks loose on earth. The antichrist deceives the masses and leads the people to become puppets for his hideous purposes. As an evil leader with evil intentions, he leads the people to do evil acts and kill each other. Though he rides on a white horse, the motives of his heart are blackened by his lust for power. Absent God's people and the work of the Holy Spirit—since both have been raptured from the earth—the world is void of peace.

—❧—

"In all this you greatly rejoice, though now
for a little while you may have had to suffer
grief in all kinds of trials" (1 Peter 1:6).

But what about your present trials? Christ's care provides a cup of refreshing water for your parched soul. It is for the love of Jesus that you persevere. Be patient. Allow Him to complete His work of refinement. You will love more deeply and forgive more fully. Hope is on the horizon and is already here, as Christ in you is the hope of glory. Hang on to your hope in Him and be made whole. Pain can polarize your relationship with God, or it can galvanize it in intimacy.

Let contentment overcome your ingratitude. Stare into the face of Jesus, for He is kind. He understands your plight. He is walking with you and is working through you. Allow God to channel His fiery trials into your character refinement. People will come out and watch a fire burn for God's glory. Trials are His time to shine, and He shines the brightest when the impurities are the least. Only Christ is left—He is all you want—He is all you need!

"He said, 'Look! I see four men walking around in
the fire, unbound and unharmed, and the fourth
looks like a son of the gods'" (Daniel 3:25).

How does Christ want to refine my character during my trials and temptations?

Related Readings
Deuteronomy 7:19; Zechariah 13:9; Luke 22:28; James 1:2

34

God's Peacekeeper

*Then another horse came out, a fiery red one. Its rider was
given power to take peace from the earth and to make
people kill each other. To him was given a large sword.*

REVELATION 6:4

God's peacekeeper is His Son Jesus Christ. His first provision of
peace is between God and man. When we trust Christ alone as
our Savior and Lord, we are at peace with our heavenly Father. Before
we placed our faith in Jesus, we were in conflict with the Almighty. Our
soul was restless, at odds with its Creator. But once we surrender our selfish ways, we enjoy peace with God—and the peace of God in our hearts.
We look to Jesus alone as our keeper of the peace. His gift is the rest His
grace provides.

The antichrist will offer a counterfeit peace that looks good on the
surface. It is alluring and exciting, but it only offers a temporary escape.
In the days of tribulation on earth, Jesus describes an anxious world
obsessed over "wars and rumors of wars" (Mark 13:7). These rumblings
of a peaceless people prove to be a harbinger of what's to come: world
war, famine, and judgment. A promise of outward control offers a false
sense of serenity, but only Jesus gives inner peace.

"He walked with me in peace and uprightness,
and turned many from sin" (Malachi 2:6).

The peace of Jesus gives us peace with ourselves. The guilt of past sin is gone. If we shame ourselves over issues Christ has already covered by His thorough cleansing, we sin. The demons of guilt have no jurisdiction over the Justice of the Peace—Jesus! Trusting in Him empowers our souls. When we behold our Prince of Peace in uninterrupted worship, we receive His radical, peace-loving assurance. Our peacekeeper Jesus is our loyal ally. Our flesh mopes around afraid, but we have no need to fear since Jesus is near. He is our peace!

Christ can even make your enemies be at peace with you. They may not believe what you believe, but they will notice and respect your steadfast faith. Your love and respect toward others is a peace offering God uses to extend His grace. The calm Christ puts within you is a testimony for those in turmoil. A person who acknowledges their anxious heart is a prime candidate for the peace of God. Stay surrendered to your Savior, and your peaceful presence will draw others to Him— as God's peacekeeper, Jesus Christ, settles your soul.

∾

"Let the peace of Christ rule in your
hearts" (Colossians 3:15).

Do I truly trust in my Savior Jesus to guard my heart and mind with His peace?

Related Readings
Numbers 6:26; Proverbs 16:7; John 14:27; Philippians 4:7

35

Fear of Death

∞∞∞

*When he opened the fifth seal, I saw under the altar
the souls of those who had been slain because of the
word of God and the testimony they had maintained.*

REVELATION 6:9

Jesus has conquered death; therefore, followers of Jesus need not fear death. You may have a fear of dying but not of death. For the believer in Christ, death is a pass-through, a transition from this life to the next. Death is not final, for it is the doorway to eternity. Eternity is being in the physical presence of Jesus. Everything we have experienced with Christ on earth is an appetizer of what is to come. Faith can only digest a mere morsel of what God has in store for those who love Him.

John honors those who sacrifice their lives on the altar of the Lord's love—such as Abel, the first martyr (Genesis 4:10; Hebrews 11:4). They died because of the transforming love of Christ dwelling in them. Courageous heroes of the faith do not compromise the truth of God's Word, nor do they betray their loyal testimony to Jesus. Death releases us from the pain of suffering, which molds our character and faith in Christ. Jesus replaces fear of death with hope in heaven.

∞∞∞

"We have heard of your faith in Christ Jesus and
of the love you have for all God's people—the
faith and love that spring from the hope stored
up for you in heaven" (Colossians 1:4-5).

Death is freedom and is not to be feared. So, in the meantime, make every effort to prepare yourself and others for death. The fear of death creeps in where there has been no preparation. You can ignore its reality, but you will still die. You can deny death but not its consequences. You may have a chance to repent on your deathbed, but why wait? Go with God's sure thing—faith in Christ. He has died and risen from the dead to give you life, and faith overcomes fear.

The depth of wisdom that comes from the dying has the aroma of heaven. The expectation of death helps us to purify our priorities and evaluate our lives. Being with the dying and caring for them prepares you for your own moment of death. Death is an absolute. It may come suddenly or at the end of a long process, but either way, we know God can be trusted. God is good, and God is great. Because Jesus died and rose again, you will do the same. Fear only God and trust Christ.

—⚬⚬⚬—

"'Death has been swallowed up in victory.' Where,
O death, is your victory?…But thanks be to
God! He gives us the victory through our Lord
Jesus Christ" (1 Corinthians 15:54-55,57).

Heavenly Father, may I die to whatever is not of You so I can live with You in eternity.

Related Readings
Matthew 27:52; Mark 8:35; John 12:23-25; 1 Corinthians 15:42-58

36

Judgment of Christ

◦∞◦

*Hide us from the face of him who sits on the
throne and from the wrath of the Lamb! For
the great day of their wrath has come.*

REVELATION 6:16-17

There are posers who profess to know God, but He will one day say to them, "I never knew you" (Matthew 7:23). It is scary to think individuals can believe they are okay with the Lord when they are not. Maybe they heard the truth of the cross, but they did not receive the truth by faith into their heart. They have never fully traded their trust in themselves for a total dependence on Christ. Faithless fools may have good religious feelings, but they have not surrendered to the convicting power of the Holy Spirit.

John describes the coming judgment of Christ. No one is excluded: Kings, princes, generals, the rich, the mighty, and everyone else must give an account of their life on earth. Fearful of God's wrath, they call to the mountains and rocks to fall and cover them from the coming peril. In the end as in the beginning, sin causes mankind to try to hide from the Lord—a frivolous and naive response. The alternative is owning and repenting of our sin. Christ's judgment exposes unsaved souls.

◦∞◦

"This is how it will be at the end of the age. The
angels will come and separate the wicked
from the righteous" (Matthew 13:49).

It is uncomfortable to picture a loving God having a system of judgment that includes hell. However, would He really be loving if He did not punish sin and reveal religious hypocrites for pretending to be something they're not? We water down the Word of God when we feel obligated to apologize for the Lord's consequences. Oh how He loves us, because on Judgment Day, wrongs will be made right in His sight.

In the meantime, pray for those who genuinely believe they are right with God but have yet to be born again. Teach those who are religious but lost about submission to the Lord and the desperate desire for Him that follows. Help fellow church members move from a head full of knowledge to a heart full of passion. Information about Jesus comes alive when Jesus is experienced in a personal, loving, and intimate relationship. Ask the Holy Spirit to flush out impostors today, before it is too late for them to change. Trust Jesus as Savior and avoid Him as Judge.

―――――∞∞∞―――――

"If you declare with your mouth, 'Jesus is Lord,' and believe in your heart that God raised him from the dead, you will be saved" (Romans 10:9).

Heavenly Father, lead me into a genuine relationship with You through Your Son Jesus.

Related Readings
Zephaniah 1:14-15; Matthew 25:32; 1 Corinthians 14:21; Revelation 20:15

37

Protected by Angels

—— ∞∞∞ ——

After this I saw four angels standing at the four
corners of the earth, holding back the four winds
of the earth to prevent any wind from blowing
on the land or on the sea or on any tree.

REVELATION 7:1

Angels are at our heavenly Father's beckoning. They are poised to support, protect, and care for His children at His prompting. Jesus could have called on a company of heavenly help, but He resisted and remained in the crucible of the cross. He had an escape route for His suffering; however, His great love led Him to sacrifice His life and save mankind from sin. God's angel armies minister to our needs, but they may or may not deliver us from harm.

The Lord will deploy His angels to delay judgment in order for the 144,000 Jewish believers in Jesus to be sealed as servants of God. The destruction of the earth is stayed until souls are saved—their white robes cleansed by the blood of the Lamb. The elder explained to John how these Jewish Christians were survivors of the great tribulation—but now they gratefully serve God day and night, before His throne in His temple (Revelation 7:14-15). God's angels provide personal protection.

—— ∞∞∞ ——

"See that you do not despise one of these little ones.
For I tell you that their angels in heaven always see
the face of my Father in heaven" (Matthew 18:10).

Your Father in heaven has angels assigned to your well-being. They constantly experience the glory of God, so they can surround you with His glory. Since your angels see the face of the Lord, they can help you face your difficulties. You have no need to fear, because the God of angel armies stands beside you, in front of you, behind you, above you, and below you. You are covered by His host of angels. Thank the Lord of hosts for His help in your time of need.

Above all, look for the angelic armies of Almighty God to defeat Satan's forces on the spiritual battlefield. Like Job, your heavenly Father's strategy may be to use your faithfulness in the middle of suffering to disarm the devil. Your obedience is oxygen to your spiritual lungs. Moreover, your angels adore the Lord with praise. Their example of genuine worship is worth emulating. Yes, your angels have God's authority to support His will for you!

<hr />

"Do you think I cannot call on my Father, and
he will at once put at my disposal more than
twelve legions of angels?" (Matthew 26:53).

In what ways are the Lord's angels protecting me and my family from present dangers?

Related Readings
Isaiah 14:12-15; Acts 12:11-23; Hebrews 1:14; 2:7-9;
Revelation 22:16

38

Do You Own a Passport?

*Before me was a great multitude that no one could
count, from every nation, tribe, people and language,
standing before the throne and before the Lamb.*

REVELATION 7:9

Christ commands Christians to go into all the world and make disciples. The Lord's vision is for all nations to come to know Him through faith in Jesus. He carries a burden to lift the burden of sin from those who need forgiveness. Our heavenly Father wants all people around the globe to hear the good news of Jesus and to grow in a personal relationship with Him. Disciples are made by hearing the gospel, believing, and obeying Christ's commands. Is your faith expression landlocked for fear of leaving your comfort zone? Have you experienced the joy of taking Jesus to the shores beyond your borders?

Heaven will be populated with people from every tribe and tongue because of people who faithfully carried the gospel to faraway places. The evangelist John paints a portrait of diverse ethnicity in eternity—one result of 144,000 Jewish witnesses taking the gospel of Jesus to the ends of the earth. The Lord's love reaches beyond all geographic borders to bring all cultures to Christ.

*"I will also make you a light for the
Gentiles, that my salvation may reach to
the ends of the earth" (Isaiah 49:6).*

Jesus states very clearly that He accompanies us as we go forth by faith to share His love. He energizes. He empowers. He engages. His Spirit invites the lost to Himself. His overseas mission mobilization is not limited to the few "navy seals" of the faith. All disciples are called to make disciples. Those who undertake cross-cultural missions need spiritual preparation and we should minister to those in our own homes before exporting our faith to foreign families. Our first priority is to live out what we believe with those who know us the best.

Moreover, manage your money well, so debt is not an obstacle to obeying God. Be free from the shackles of financial entrapment, so you are free to serve the Lord in different time zones. Perhaps you start with a short-term mission trip to "test the waters." In fact, most people will not be called to a permanent overseas assignment in disciple making, but many can travel for a time. Obtain a passport so you can be ready to follow Christ's command and make disciples of all nations.

———— ⊱⊰ ————

"You will be my witnesses in Jerusalem, and in all Judea and Samaria, and to the ends of the earth" (Acts 1:8).

Heavenly Father, grow me into a faithful disciple, so I can make disciples of all nations.

Related Readings
1 Chronicles 16:8; Zechariah 2:11; Matthew 28:19-20; Acts 13:47

39

Live This Life for the Next Life

⤬

They cried out in a loud voice: "Salvation belongs to our God, who sits on the throne."

REVELATION 7:9-10

This life is preparation for the next life. Those who live only for this brief time on earth will one day wake up to a joyless eternity, but those who live intentionally for the next life will experience a joyful eternity. The object of our focus determines the level of our fulfillment. Focusing on God and others protects us from being consumed by petty personal issues. Deeply satisfied Christians invest their lives in selfless service. Intentional living praises God.

John describes a scene in heaven reminiscent of the Jewish custom of celebration during harvest time. Many had faithfully tilled the soil, planted the seeds, and cultivated the tender plants, while God provided the growing conditions of rain and sunshine. Cooperation with the divine agenda reaped the Lord's abundant provision. In addition, people celebrated the Lord's past faithfulness. Walking with Jesus on earth is a lifelong apprenticeship for the worship of Jesus for eternity in heaven. Joy is a choice!

⤬

"As a result, they do not live the rest of their earthly lives for evil human desires, but rather for the will of God" (1 Peter 4:2).

Is your rudder custom crafted by the love of Christ, or are you rudderless and adrift on the rough sea of life? When the Spirit guides you, He gives you life. If God is your guide, you will go places with Him that are impossible without Him. This is the joy of doing life *with* Jesus—not busily doing life *for* Jesus. The Holy Spirit's rhythm of life is not without challenges, but He is in harmony with what's best. At the core of His calling are joy, peace, and worship.

What areas of your life need prayerful intentionality? Pursuing a relationship with Christ feeds your soul, humbles your heart, and expands your mind. Spending time every day with the Truth and the Life will nurture your wisdom and bring light to your life. Your investment of time and energy into people and God's Word will last forever, so being intentional with those who do not know Jesus reaps joy on earth and rejoicing in heaven. Do you know some people who need the Lord? Are you praying for them? Intentional love saves souls.

"The kingdom of heaven is like a treasure hidden in a field. When a man found it, he hid it again, and then in his joy went and sold all he had and bought that field" (Matthew 13:44).

Who in my life doesn't know the Lord? How can I be Jesus to them?

Related Readings
Psalm 145:7; Isaiah 49:13; Luke 10:20; Romans 12:12; Colossians 1:12

40

A God Hug

*The Lamb at the center of the throne will be their
shepherd; "he will lead them to springs of living water."
"And God will wipe away every tear from their eyes."*

REVELATION 7:17

A God hug is a timely gift. His hugs soothe, comfort, and calm. He is never late in offering His affection or too busy to stand still and embrace His human creation. The Spirit gently caresses burdened and painful shoulders. His compassion has never failed. His mercy is fresh every day. As a cool cream alleviates an itchy skin rash, so His balm of grace relieves a rash of worries. A God hug holds on until healing occurs. He holds on tight.

Jesus is the Great Shepherd who will tenderly lead His sheep to springs of living water. Though the sovereign Judge and the Lion of Judah, Jesus also cares for His sheep, whose hearts are heavy and hurting. Tears trickle into the hands of the One who holds the world and who wipes away weeping with His gentle touch. Sheep who look to their compassionate Shepherd for care will not despair, but take comfort in His secure affection.

*"The LORD comforts his people and will have
compassion on his afflicted ones" (Isaiah 49:13).*

A God hug does not happen on the run, but while we stand still. "Slow down, My child," He says. "Hush. I have this. Be still, and let Me hold you. Rest in My arms." We must learn to stand still sometimes and trust the right activities will get done in the right time. When we schedule time for the Lord to express His love to us, we receive strength for the journey. Otherwise we exhaust our ability to encourage, lacking an infusion of Christ's courage. His hugs hearten us. The Lord comforts us so we can comfort others.

Shout for joy in praise to your Creator for His comfort and compassion. Brag on His name and extol Him for His divine affection. Like the father of the prodigal son who came home, your Father in heaven can't wait to embrace you in your shame, stress, or success. He runs to greet you with warm acceptance, so throw yourself into His arms. Cast your cares on Christ and abandon your life to the Lord. Welcome His affections and enjoy His sweet embrace!

"I will turn their mourning into gladness; I will give them comfort and joy instead of sorrow" (Jeremiah 31:13).

Heavenly Father, I receive Your love and affection. Thanks for Your comforting hugs just when I need them.

Related Readings
Psalm 23:4; Jeremiah 8:18; Zechariah 10:2; 2 Corinthians 1:3-4

41

Moment of Silence

⊸⊸⊸⊸

When he opened the seventh seal, there was
silence in heaven for about half an hour.

REVELATION 8:1

Sometimes silence is the best strategy. How good does it feel to trade your exhausting striving for some energizing silence? Our flesh wants to engage in an emotional debate, but our spirit says wait. When we pause for the Holy Spirit to calm our conflicted hearts, we will be better equipped for confronting the issues before us. Our daily battles are best fought when faith in Jesus is at the forefront. A person may agitate us, but by God's grace, we can refrain from a rude reaction and pray for them. We won't allow another's bad day to ruin our day. God can speak clearly when we are quiet and patient.

Heaven grew silent for 30 minutes in awe of God Almighty and in a solemn moment of respect for the imminent destruction of earth and its inhabitants. Evil is eventually and fully judged, and secret sins or blatant bad behavior will encounter crushing consequences. Even the morally good people who rejected Jesus Christ as Lord and Savior will regret their choice. Heaven's silence precedes earth's loud obliteration.

⊸⊸⊸⊸

"This is what the Sovereign LORD, the Holy One
of Israel, says: 'In repentance and rest is your
salvation, in quietness and trust is your strength,
but you would have none of it'" (Isaiah 30:15).

Our flesh screams for its way, but we must remain silent with respect. Our words may delay the work of God's Word. For example, if someone we know is seeking wisdom from their heavenly Father, better to pray with them than to assume we know what they need to do. Instead of prescribing a solution for them based on our own experience, we can refer them to Scriptures relevant to their situation. God speaks through His Word.

Our silence invites the Lord's inner strength into our souls. Patience grows in an environment of trust. Instead of saying something we later regret, we can wait on the Spirit to speak into the situation. He may impress humility on our hearts or forgiveness on the hearts of those we've let down. God can use another caring believer to bring clarity to the confusion or a solution to the problem. Surrender to Christ and invite Him to fight for you. Your silence releases His resources.

"The LORD will fight for you while you
keep silent" (Exodus 14:14 NASB).

Heavenly Father, in my silence I hope to hear Your voice and submit my will to Yours.

Related Readings
1 Samuel 17:47; Psalms 24:8; 35:1; Matthew 26:63; Acts 15:12

42

Prayer for God's Purposes

❦

The smoke of the incense, together with the prayers of
God's people, went up before God from the angel's hand.

REVELATION 8:4

Prayer is not meant to be perfunctory, but powered by the Holy Spirit. When I am preoccupied and trying to pray, I short-circuit the Spirit's work. However, when I pray in the Spirit, I experience full contact with Christ; my mind is engaged, and my heart is fully focused. The flesh seeks a quick fix, but the Spirit desires a deep affection that develops over time. Spiritual prayers flow from praise and worship to Almighty God. He receives the prayer aroma from His daughters and sons as the sweet smell of a holy sacrifice. The Holy Spirit is our prayer whisperer.

Prayers for justice in this life may not be answered until the next life. Like incense, the prayers of God's people waft up into the nostrils of God. The altar normally designed for mercy is repurposed for justice. As the prayers of the saints in heaven ascend to the Lord, the Lord's judgment descends on the earth and its inhabitants. Without consequences for evil, grace and mercy lose their luster. Yes, prayer and faith facilitate God's purposes into action.

❦

"Pray in the Spirit on all occasions with all kinds
of prayers and requests" (Ephesians 6:18).

Pray on all occasions. With a bowed head, recognize Jesus as the provider of a delicious meal. Before you partake of the tasty morsels, taste His grace. Pray and prepare your heart prior to a difficult conversation, so any anger or harshness gives way to patience and compassion. Pray as you think about a big decision, asking, "Is my motive to glorify God? What counsel would I give to someone else in a similar situation?" Spiritual prayers have the Spirit's leading.

Variety is the spice of an effective prayer life. Yes, employ a plethora of prayers that protect you from familiarity and boredom. Pray for patience so you are slow to anger. Pray for the sick so they might be healed. Pray for opportunities to share the gospel so the seeds of salvation will grow in the hearts of lost souls. Pray for those who suffer so their comfort comes from Christ. Pray for forgiveness so your heart is healed and filled with the Holy Spirit!

―――∞∞∞―――

"I pray that out of his glorious riches he may
strengthen you with power through his Spirit
in your inner being" (Ephesians 3:16).

Heavenly Father, I pray that my prayers are full of praise and thanksgiving to You.

Related Readings
Isaiah 11:2; Micah 3:8; Mark 14:38; Acts 4:31; Colossians 1:9; Jude 20

43

Delayed Repentance Escalates Discipline

*The first angel sounded his trumpet, and there came
hail and fire mixed with blood, and it was hurled down
on the earth. A third of the earth was burned up.*

REVELATION 8:7

Spiritual fruit from the past is no substitute for fruit produced in the present. Praise God for our faithful ancestors of the faith, but their fruit was for their time. The Spirit of God wants to harvest fruits of repentance for this generation. The good old days of spiritual renewal are inspiring, but today the Lord calls those of us with a little gray hair to grow up in His grace. We who identify with Jesus have a significant role and responsibility to produce fruit of repentance.

Those who do not bear fruit in this life will experience the severe discipline of the Lord in the next life. Indeed, as we close in on Christ's second coming, we must be prepared to meet our Maker with lives that reflect God's standards, not the anemic morality of a sick society. A world that rejects Jesus and refuses to repent of sin is not a pretty sight. The discipline of the Lord will escalate across a scorched earth.

"Godly sorrow brings repentance that leads
to salvation and leaves no regret, but worldly
sorrow brings death" (2 Corinthians 7:10).

How do we know if we are producing fruit of repentance? Private belief for salvation and public confession in baptism are the firstfruits of repentance, but they are only the beginning. The ongoing fruit-bearing process is a lifetime of leaning into the Lord. The Spirit reminds us when we drift into bad habits or wrong thinking. We confess spiritual pride and remember that only by the grace of God can we do good. We turn from self-righteousness and toward God's righteousness.

What is the fruit of repentance? Good deeds from a heart of humility and grace are fruits that glorify God. Your Spirit-filled actions of abstinence, generosity, tutoring, public service, faith sharing, foster care, and orphan adoption please your heavenly Father. Jesus smiles when you are hospitable and when you visit the sick and those in prison. Your authentic repentance compels you to care for the broken. What breaks God's heart breaks your heart!

"I preached that they should repent and turn
to God and demonstrate their repentance
by their deeds" (Acts 26:20).

From what must I repent, turning to the Lord for forgiveness and the faith to produce good deeds?

Related Readings
Deuteronomy 4:30; Jeremiah 18:11; Luke 3:8-9; Galatians 3:7

44

Possessed by God

*They were told not to harm the grass of the earth
or any plant or tree, but only those people who did
not have the seal of God on their foreheads.*

REVELATION 9:4

Our Savior's seal is a picture of His possession of us and our relationship with Him. What a deal: We surrender ourselves, and in exchange we know God, we have access to Him, and He owns us. What the Holy Spirit has, He preserves. He is our guarantee. Our inheritance is a secure life with Jesus now and forever. God's rich grace gives us the commerce to build His kingdom. We are sealed by the Lord, driven by His will and purpose.

John makes clear those who are sealed by God are under His protection. The final days of judgment will pass over the people who have placed their faith in Christ, but those who have trusted in their own version of truth will be found out. They will miss out on the rewards of a grace-filled life. Unbelievers will wish they had trusted and followed the promise of Jesus to possess His power that overcomes (Luke 10:19).

"You are a chosen people, a royal priesthood, a
holy nation, God's special possession, that you may
declare the praises of him who called you out of
darkness into his wonderful light" (1 Peter 2:9).

What does it mean to be in relationship with the Lord? We have intimate access to Abba God. We seek our heavenly Father in faith and quiet confidence. He is gracious and gives us strength for life's journey. We walk with our Savior Jesus, who, like a compassionate big brother, forgives us, cares for us, and calls us friends. We follow the Holy Spirit away from temptation and into the Lord's will. As blessed children of God, we have all we need!

What does it mean to be possessed by the Lord? What God possesses He keeps. He keeps us as His own. He is jealous of other suitors, so He keeps us as His special people. He loves the world, but He loves with everlasting love those who trust His Son Jesus Christ as their Lord and Savior. He keeps us for His praise and glory. When we sing to our great and majestic Almighty God, it is a holy and acceptable sacrifice to heaven. He protects and prizes His sealed children.

"When you believed, you were marked in him with a seal, the promised Holy Spirit, who is a deposit guaranteeing our inheritance until the redemption of those who are God's possession" (Ephesians 1:13-14).

Heavenly Father, thank You for Your rich inheritance and for possessing my life.

Related Readings
Deuteronomy 7:6; 1 Samuel 12:22; Romans 9:25-26; Titus 2:12-14

45

Shadow of Death

*During those days people will seek death but will not
find it; they will long to die, but death will elude them.*

REVELATION 9:6

Everyone walks through life in the long shadow of death. There is no part of the globe where it can be avoided and no physical condition that it can escape. Death knocks on the doors of all demographics, all cultures, and all classes of people. During the great tribulation, however—because of intense suffering—some will seek death but be unable to die. Part of their torment will be prolonged pain without the presence of God to comfort them. Death will elude the unsaved.

Death can bring discomfort, discouragement, and even despair. Amid the valley of death, faith is tested, families are stressed, and friends rally in prayer. How do you serve someone who is living their last months or days on earth? A good first step is to be an example of faith for them. A dying loved one needs love from those who know the Lord so that they can come to know the Lord too. A dying person needs care, comfort, and heaven's hope. Allow death to bring you together as a family, as it did for Saul and his son Jonathan.

"Saul and Jonathan—in life they were
loved and admired, and in death they
were not parted" (2 Samuel 1:23).

Death is God's reminder that we need Him and we need each other. We all walk toward death—but in Christ, death becomes a passage to eternal life. We may suffer when a believing parent begins to lose their ability to think clearly, but we can patiently listen to their irrational words knowing one day they will speak with tongues of angels. If a parent lacks belief, we can pray the reality of death brings them to the Lord.

Our faith in Jesus triumphs over death, and it also comforts us along the way. The destination of this life is death, but when we travel with the Lord, we need not fear evil or the unknown. His presence is all we need to persevere in righteous living. Hope, peace, and love are the outflow of walking with Jesus through the lonely valley of death. Death is a pass-through to paradise, for the cross is a comfort to the dying and a bridge to heaven for those who believe in Jesus's death, His resurrection, and an eternal life in heaven.

"Even though I walk through the darkest valley, I
will fear no evil, for you are with me" (Psalm 23:4).

Am I walking through my valleys with Jesus? With whom can I walk through their valley?

Related Readings
Psalm 56:13; Isaiah 38:10; John 5:24; Romans 8:38

46

Influence of Impure Spirits

※

*The rest of mankind who were not killed by these
plagues still did not repent of the work of their
hands; they did not stop worshiping demons.*

REVELATION 9:20

Impure spirits live inside some people, even in our places of worship. Satan is their master, and they are set on disrupting the work of God. They may say they believe in God because "even the demons believe and tremble," but their hearts are far from Him. Impure spirits try to blend in with true believers, but they are exposed as fakes to those with spiritual discernment. Christ's presence drives them out.

Jesus encountered evil in the synagogue and cast out the impure spirit from the man (Mark 1:23-26). Demons are not comfortable where Christ is taught and where the Spirit of God has a powerful presence. Unfortunately, some impotent churches have people who go through the motions with zombielike spiritual energy. In the days of God's great judgment, some people will continue to stubbornly worship demons. Impure spirits lead people to live impure lives.

※

"You believe that there is one God. Good! Even the
demons believe that—and shudder" (James 2:19).

Therefore, make sure not to make light of the influence of impure spirits. If you embrace activities and entertainments that espouse evil, you expose yourself and your family to the influence of impure spirits.

Even fun activities and jests can open the door to the unintentional consequences of accepting the abnormal as normal. Your children can dress up and have fun without imitating witches, warlocks, spiritists, and the occult. Why dance with the enemy and risk defilement by his influence?

Furthermore, pray against impure spirits in the pure name of Jesus Christ. They cannot stand it when we stand up to them in His mighty name. Everyone will bow to our Lord Jesus.

> Therefore God exalted him to the highest place and gave him the name that is above every name, that at the name of Jesus every knee should bow, in heaven and on earth and under the earth, and every tongue acknowledge that Jesus Christ is Lord, to the glory of God the Father (Philippians 2:9-11).

Impure spirits cannot remain in the presence of purity, which is embodied by the Lord Jesus.

"Do not turn to mediums or seek out spiritists, for you will be defiled by them. I am the LORD your God" (Leviticus 19:31).

Heavenly Father, lead me by Your Spirit to discern impure spirits and confront them in the pure name of Jesus Christ.

Related Readings
1 Samuel 28:3-9; Job 1:6-12; Mark 3:13-15; 1 Timothy 4:1; Revelation 9:20

47

God's Ways Fulfilled

*In the days when the seventh angel is about to sound
his trumpet, the mystery of God will be accomplished,
just as he announced to his servants the prophets.*

REVELATION 10:7

Our gracious God grants us wisdom in His ways. He wants us to experience His eternal aim for His glory. When we placed our faith in Jesus, His purpose was partially fulfilled. Our contract with Christ laid the responsibility of fulfilling His full purpose at the feet of our heavenly Father. Our Lord finishes what He begins. Whatsoever the Lord takes in hand, He will accomplish, so we trust the Almighty to fulfill His plan.

The mystery of God's plan had already been announced to His servants, the prophets. They prophesied the first coming of Jesus as a suffering servant for the sins of mankind, and Christ's second coming as reigning King and Judge. Without faith, the ways of the Lord remain a mystery, but by faith God's children are able to see God's ways. Faith brings complete fulfillment.

"Being confident of this, that he who began a
good work in you will carry it on to completion
until the day of Christ Jesus" (Philippians 1:6).

Prayer prepares us to harvest heaven's purpose for our life. We cry out to the Most High because there is nothing and no one any higher.

God, who made us, is the divine decision maker. Nowhere else can we go to understand the purpose of our lives other than the Lord Jesus Christ. We cry out to Christ because He has adopted us. Our heavenly Father defines our purpose, and prayer positions us to be led by the Holy Spirit. He finishes what He begins.

Lean into the Lord, letting Him lead you toward His plan for your life. Once you establish His purpose for you, leverage it for others. Use your strength of position to help others discover their God-given purpose. Talk to them about their gifts, skills, passions, and experiences. Pray with them about how God wants to collate their assets for Christ.

No season of life is insignificant in the Lord's eyes. Don't wish away where you are today. By faith, you can be sure that Christ is currently working through you. Make sure your goals are God-given and trust Him with their fulfillment!

———— ∞ ————

"I cry out to God Most High, to God who will
fulfill his purpose for me" (Psalm 57:2 NLT).

What is the role of prayer in fulfilling God's plan? How can I adjust my goals to reflect God's?

Related Readings
1 Chronicles 28:12; Job 5:11-12; Psalms 20:4; 33:11;
2 Corinthians 1:15-18

48

Internalize Scripture

I took the little scroll from the angel's hand and
ate it. It tasted as sweet as honey in my mouth, but
when I had eaten it, my stomach turned sour.

REVELATION 10:10

Memorizing Scripture is an effective defense against sin, Satan, and self. It is also God's primary method of conforming us into the image of His Son Jesus Christ. We all are privileged to renew our minds with the truth of Scripture and to cleanse our hearts with the purifying Word of God. Were we to commit to memory a verse a week related to what we are experiencing in life, over the course of a year we would hide 52 nuggets of spiritual nourishment within our souls. "I have hidden your word in my heart that I might not sin against you" (Psalm 119:11).

Similar to Ezekiel (2:9; 3:1-3), John is instructed to eat the scroll (God's Word). It tastes sweet to him, but to those who have to stomach the Lord's judgment, it will taste sour. John well understood sorrow and suffering after living out the reality of being rejected for the testimony of Jesus. He experienced the application and transformation of God's Word.

"The LORD continued to appear at Shiloh,
and there he revealed himself to Samuel
through his word" (1 Samuel 3:21).

The Lord reveals Himself through His Word. As the Word makes its way into the crevices of our character, we increasingly desire to know God, love God, and obey God. We are conformed by the character of Christ as we mature in our understanding of the Word made flesh. Yes, we grow in our love for the Word and for Christ Himself, the living Word who was revealed on earth. God's secret weapon of memorized, internalized Scripture transforms us into the likeness of Christ.

We are wise to see the memorizing of Scripture memory as a blessing, not a burden. Be creative. We can listen to God's Word as we commute to work, exercise, or do chores around the house. We can follow Jesus's example by seamlessly saying to Satan, "It is written." God's Word written on our hearts through memorization and meditation equips us to stand strong in Him. The spiritual growth plan of hiding His Word is used by seasoned saints who deeply know and love the Lord.

"How can a young person stay on the path of purity?
By living according to your word" (Psalm 119:9).

Heavenly Father, help me hide Your Word in my heart that I might know You, love You, and obey You.

Related Readings
Psalm 19:14; Jeremiah 15:16; Matthew 4:1-11; John 1:14; Ephesians 6:17

49

Appointed by God

─────◆◇◆─────

*I will appoint my two witnesses, and they will
prospesy for 1,260 days, clothed in sackcloth.*

REVELATION 11:3

The Lord seeks out disciples who are sensitive to His heart—those ready and willing to follow His next appointment to witness and serve. God seeks sincere seekers whom He can entrust with His favor. He recruits submissive star players for His team, so let your heart rest in the hand of your heavenly Father. You will endure under the mighty hand of the Almighty. Outside of His authority, hope shrivels and help fades away, so gladly accept God's next appointment.

Just as Jesus sent out His disciples in pairs, so the Lord appoints two witnesses to proclaim His truth for three and a half years. Empowered by the Holy Spirit, these bold prophets will have the ability to destroy their enemies and cause plagues to infect the earth as evidence of God's presence and mankind's stubborn heart. Once the two witnesses finish their assignment from heaven, the beast will arise from hell to attack, overpower, and kill them. What the devil deems as dead, the Spirit is able to bring back to life. Divine appointments may die to be revived again.

─────◆◇◆─────

"The LORD has sought out a man after his own heart and
appointed him ruler of his people" (1 Samuel 13:14).

Keep your heart tender toward God by constantly cultivating the commands of Christ. You remain useful to your heavenly Father by staying sensitive to the Spirit's service appointments. The Lord is not looking at your outward appearance, but at your inward beauty and integrity. Perhaps your mind needs cleansing, so pray with submission for renewal in the Spirit. Also, keep your pride in check with humble acts of service at home.

Because the Holy Spirit seeks you out, you are wise to turn toward Him and move in His direction. Obedience to God will move you toward Him, while disobedience to God will always move you away. The Lord may be seeking you to replace another unwilling servant of His, so remain humble as opportunities to serve Him open up. Your added responsibilities make you more responsible to represent Christ well. Surrender to God's search for your heart.

<hr/>

"Submit to God and be at peace with him; in this
way prosperity will come to you" (Job 22:21).

I am available and willing to follow God's appointments to humbly serve and witness for Him. With whom can I partner in kingdom-minded ministry?

Related Readings
2 Chronicles 30:8; Isaiah 26:12; John 4:23; Philippians 3:3

50

Evil for Good

—⦿—

The inhabitants of the earth will gloat over them and will
celebrate by sending each other gifts, because these two
prophets had tormented those who live on the earth.

REVELATION 11:10

Sometimes a good deed can result in the opposite of what we expect—an evil reaction. People we have served seem to have forgotten our faithfulness, and gratitude has faded from their memory. They have forgotten the fruit of our labors, and it has become all about what might inconvenience them. You were there for them at their point of need, but now in your need, they reject your request. It seems like a cruel joke. How could they forget your love and loyalty?

What do you do when you are repaid evil for good? What is your prayerful response?

The only prophet an unbelieving world likes is a dead prophet, so for three and a half days, contempt is shown for the two bold witnesses of Christ. Their corpses are left unburied in the street—an insult to God and His spokesmen. A celebration breaks out in honor of the antichrist, who has temporarily quieted the pesky and persistent voices of truth. This occasion for rejoicing during the tribulation is an aberration—not seen before or after. God eventually makes right the shamelessness of evil's ugly acts in His sight.

—⦿—

"It's been useless—all my watching over
this fellow's property in the desert so that

nothing of his was missing. He has paid me
back evil for good" (1 Samuel 25:21).

When evil intent is injected into a relationship, we must resist firing back with equally evil actions. We cannot lower ourselves to this kind of schoolyard revenge. The question is not, "What is the right thing for them to do?" The question is, "What is the right thing for me to do?" You can reverse the force of the verbal jabs by returning good for evil. When you choose not to fight false accusations by accosting your accuser, you repay good for evil.

The Lord Almighty can take care of evil people and their actions. Wait on Him to settle matters as He sees fit, especially if you have the option to hurt someone. Trust Christ to deal with them in His timing. Evildoers may never change, but they might. It is a heart issue between them and God. In the meantime, when you encounter evil, repay it with good and trust Jesus. The goodness of God trumps evil, for evil is no match for God's goodness.

———— ✨ ————

"If you repay good with evil, evil will never
leave your house" (Proverbs 17:13 NLT).

What good deed has a friend done that needs my positive support in the face of unfair criticism?

Related Readings

Genesis 44:4; 1 Samuel 19:4; Psalm 35:12; 1 Peter 3:17

51

Revived by God

～∞∞～

*After the three and a half days the breath of life
from God entered them, and they stood on their
feet, and terror struck those who saw them.*

REVELATION 11:11

A once-thriving spiritual life can go unconscious. As with a lifeless body on an emergency room gurney, a sudden shock of the heart is needed to revive the temporarily deceased. If someone's faith emits only a faint pulse, they need a jolt. The Lord loves His children too much to leave them in a disconnected spiritual state. His breath fills a faithful follower's lungs with fresh air.

Holy God brings His holy prophets back to life by breathing life into their lungs, similar to the way His breath revived dry bones so many centuries earlier (Ezekiel 37:1-14). As the resurrected servants of God stand to their feet, terror strikes those who thought the truth tellers had been snuffed out, not to be heard from again. But with only a moment's notice, the Lord calls His servants to ascend in a cloud to heaven as earth's inhabitants remained terrified.

———∞∞———

"I live in a high and holy place, but also with
the one who is contrite and lowly in spirit, to
revive the spirit of the lowly and to revive
the heart of the contrite" (Isaiah 57:15).

A humble and contrite heart unleashes Christ's love into a spiritual life. Therefore we humbly approach holy God, who is high and lifted up and who longs to lift up our prayers of repentance and rejoicing. Our heavenly Father is drawn to our desperate need for Him. He reaches out with both hands, lays them on our heads, and renews our minds with His truth. We call on His name because He is worthy of our worship and because we need His face to shine on us.

Do you need a jolt from Jesus to bring your faith back to life? When our spiritual life is revived, we turn away from sin and toward the Lord. Perhaps your appetite for God is starved and needs an intravenous line of love from the Lord Almighty to restore your spiritual life. Engage the Holy Spirit with a humble spirit, and He will revive you. Seek Christ with a contrite heart, and He will restore the joy of your salvation. God revives so we can thrive for Him!

<hr />

"They will see God's face and shout for joy; he will restore them to full well-being" (Job 33:26).

Heavenly Father, revive my spirit to follow Your Spirit, and give me spiritual life through Your life.

Related Readings
Psalms 51:10-12; 80:18-19; Hosea 6:2; Acts 3:21; 1 Peter 5:10

52

Pride Comes Before a Fall

∞∞∞

*That ancient serpent called the devil, or Satan,
who leads the whole world astray. He was
hurled to the earth, and his angels with him.*

REVELATION 12:9

A pedestal of pride looks down on what it deems "inferior souls."
Pride is a position of self-worship that threatens integrity and influence. Like a drug, pride is addictive and impairs good judgment. If it could be packaged as a pill in a prescription bottle, the label would read, "Warning: taken too often in large doses may lead to a great fall, even death." If we don't wake up from a narcissistic dream, it can turn into a hellish nightmare. Relationships will be wrecked, and reputations will be ruined.

Similar to the serpent in the Garden of Eden, the shifty devil is an enemy to the woman and all who are under her influence. The dragon (Satan) tries to devour the woman's son, but He is protected by God and exalted to His heavenly throne (Revelation 12:4-5). This war in heaven, prompted by Satan's desire to usurp God's authority (Isaiah 14:12-15), results in his fall to earth along with a third of the angels. Pride left unchecked brings heartache and a hellish descent.

∞∞∞

"So, if you think you are standing firm, be careful
that you don't fall!" (1 Corinthians 10:12).

A prayerful posture dethrones pride and replaces it with humility. When we have faith, Jesus is able to storm the gates of hell, take captive the enemy, and release us from the prison of pride. The Lord lifts us out of the slimy pit of pride and sets us on His solid rock of righteousness. It is firm because our feet are planted on the ground of grace. Thus, we are careful to see ourselves as God sees us: needy and dependent on His Spirit.

You will stand firm by faith in Christ and trust that He is in control. Let go and let God make you whole. Let go and let the Lord take you further faster. Let go and let Christ make you content. Let go and let the Spirit show you the way. Let go and let Jesus give you joy. Approach Him with humility, and your pride will diminish. Pride has no place in the personality of a child of God. You are the result of grace alone— the Lord lifts up the humble to stand firm in Him.

———∞———

"He lifted me out of the slimy pit, out of the mud and mire; he set my feet on a rock and gave me a firm place to stand" (Psalm 40:2).

What pedestals of pride in my life need to be toppled?

Related Readings

Psalm 18:27; Proverbs 16:18; Isaiah 13:11; Romans 12:16

53

Doubt the Devil's Accusations

———— ∞∞ ————

The accuser of our brothers and sisters, who accuses them
before our God day and night, has been hurled down.

REVELATION 12:10

J ohn flushes out the true intent of the devil—the accuser of the breth-
ren whose goal is to tell lies that lead us to doubt the Lord. This
dragon of death attempts to drag everyone down with him to the
depths of hell. In an instant Satan snatched a third of the angels and
cast them out of heaven to become demonic tormentors on earth (Revelation 12:4). The devil and his demons are persistent in their accusations to discredit Christ and His followers.

Now that you have aged in years as a Christian, you may have for-
malized your faith to the point where the mundane is more likely than
the miraculous. Questions and doubt have replaced God's promises of
assurance. You ask, "Did God really say my relationship with Him is
based on my belief in Jesus Christ as His Son (John 14:6)? Did God
really say that those who believe in Jesus go to heaven, and those who
reject Him are separated from God eternally in hell (Revelation 20:15)?"

———— ∞∞ ————

"He said to the woman, 'Did God really say, "You must
not eat from any tree in the garden"?' "(Genesis 3:1).

"Did God really say that I am to pay my taxes as an example of good
citizenship (Mark 12:17)? Did God really say I am to honor my parents, even if they are undeserving of honor (Ephesians 6:1-3)? Did God

really say to volunteer in the church, start tithing, stay in this marriage, forgive my friend, invest in my family, and help my neighbor? Did He really say to trust Him, even when I don't feel Him? Am I to obey Him when I don't understand why or how?" Yes to all!

Your Lord has proven Himself time and time again as faithful and dependable. Even when you strayed, your Savior has been there when you turn back to truth. Christ is totally trustworthy. Find protection in His warnings, find assurance in His promises, and find guidance in His rules for living. Trust His track record of provision, and believe His truth will set you free. Always doubt the devil's accusations, but never doubt God's promises.

"Jesus said to him, 'Away from me, Satan! For it is written: "Worship the Lord your God, and serve him only."' Then the devil left him, and angels came and attended him" (Matthew 4:10-11).

What doubts do I need to unmask as the devil's accusations? How can I release them to God?

Related Readings
2 Chronicles 33:12; Job 36:16-19; John 20:27; Jude 22

54

Persistence Invites Persecution

*Then the dragon was enraged at the woman
and went off to wage war against the rest of her
offspring—those who keep God's commands
and hold fast their testimony about Jesus.*

REVELATION 12:17

Has rejection caused you to give up on an opportunity or a person? Are you tired of trying to do the right thing without seeing positive results? At this point of frustration and fear, God calls us to persevere in prayer, to love individuals aggressively, and to trust in the Lord. Those who give up in the face of opposition are giving up on God. Like an oscillating fan, your faith may waver back and forth between confidence and uncertainty, so hit the button of belief. Stay faithful to Jesus.

John makes clear whom the devil is most determined to target with temptation and trials: the followers of Christ who keep God's commands and who are not ashamed of their testimony. Satan is not concerned about "Christians" who have no real evidence of faith, who only go through the motions of religion without a vibrant outward expression of a deep inward work of the Holy Spirit. But the devil is enraged by a person's persistent love for God and people.

"He will give eternal life to those who patiently do the will of God, seeking for the unseen glory and honor and eternal life that he offers" (Romans 2:7 TLB).

A faithful man or woman in the hands of God has the attention of heaven and earth. It's not the individual full of energy at the outset who outlasts others; it's the wise one who applies vigor over the long haul, strengthened by the Savior's stamina. Faithful fortitude forges great relationships and gets long-term results. Anyone can start a race with excitement and anticipation, but fewer are the runners who climb the hills, overcome the adverse elements, and finish the course. You may not be the fastest—you may not finish first—but by God's grace you will finish well.

Most of all, stay persistent in prayer. Respond to God as the violin responds to the bow of the master. The Lord makes beautiful music on the strings of a life surrendered to Him. Persist through the pain of rejection and the pressures of responsibility, all the while maintaining an attitude of prayer. Persistent prayer to Jesus produces His best outcomes. Persistence pays off when you are prepared to move forward on behalf of your Master, Jesus Christ.

"Rejoice always, pray continually, give thanks in
all circumstances; for this is God's will for you
in Christ Jesus" (1 Thessalonians 5:16-18).

What relationship or opportunity calls for my focused attention and persistence?

Related Readings
Numbers 14:38; Daniel 6:10; Luke 18:1-5; Acts 20:22-25;
Romans 2:7

55

False Worshippers

*People worshiped the dragon because he had given
authority to the beast, and they also worshiped the beast.*

REVELATION 13:4

There is a false religion that has no authentic faith in Jesus Christ. People who lack a real relationship with the Lord can know all the right words to say without knowing the Word who became flesh. These fake followers of Jesus may mislead other church members, but they can't deceive Almighty God. A false faith fails for lack of focus on the true God. The beast seeks to mimic Jesus but persecutes and kills, while Jesus loves and saves.

Therefore, we are all wise to examine our hearts and ask the Holy Spirit to validate our conversion to Christ. The Spirit of our heavenly Father drew us to Himself, and the same Spirit of God affirms our faith. We do not pass from death to life by just living in a household of faith; we come to Christ by taking hold of faith in Him. Our transaction of trust in Jesus seals our future—we will be with Jesus. He keeps us secure and focused on authentic worship.

"No one can come to me unless the Father
who sent me draws them, and I will raise
them up at the last day" (John 6:44).

Are you a counterfeit follower of Christ or a true disciple? Are you sure of your salvation? If you are in doubt, seek out your Savior Jesus, who can remove your concerns. Cry to Him in confession and repentance from your sin of unbelief and embrace your Lord in fidelity of faith. Just as marriage is a public commitment of a man and woman, so your conversion is a public commitment of your total trust in Jesus. Other sincere saints who humbly seek the Lord surround you in prayer and support, and God offers assurance.

The Holy Spirit is able to flush out false worship and replace it with genuine faith in Jesus. He is able to root out unscrupulous motives and exchange them for love and obedience. Examine your heart, but more importantly, allow the Lord to do a spiritual examination. God validates your salvation on this side of death so there will be no surprises on the other side. Confess Jesus as Lord now, and there will be no doubt about your fate later. True worship of God is in the Spirit and in truth—Jesus.

—⊗∞⊗—

"God is spirit, and his worshipers must worship
in the Spirit and in truth" (John 4:24).

Heavenly Father, I trust Jesus, Lord of my life, to save my soul.

Related Readings
Hosea 8:12; Matthew 7:21-23; Romans 8:16; 10:9; Ephesians 1:17; 1 John 3:24

56

Poisonous Words

—✺—

*The beast was given a mouth to utter proud
words and blasphemies and to exercise
its authority for forty-two months.*

REVELATION 13:5

Poisonous words come from a proud heart. In our original state of sin, Satan, the old serpent, infected us with the venom of injurious words. We have to watch what we say, or we may regret it later. When people are angry, they tend to say what their parents said in their anger. It is a vicious cycle of cynicism that only Christ can break. Psalm 140:3 says, "They make their tongues as sharp as a serpent's; the poison of vipers is on their lips."

Instead of lashing out with language that stings or slanders, take time to cool down so you can think calmly and clearly. Frustration tends to feed judgmental behavior. When our throat is dry and our blood pressure is up, we do well to keep quiet instead of allowing our anger and other emotions to produce judgmental, poisonous words.

—✺—

"A gentle answer turns away wrath, but a harsh
word stirs up anger" (Proverbs 15:1).

If you have been bitten by bitter words, then apply the balm of first bowing down to Christ. Jesus has just what the wounded soul and hurting heart need. The Holy Spirit helps you discern how you can become better, and He gives you the patience, humility, and wisdom to know when to wait or when to confront. Victims of poisonous words need the serum of their Savior's love and forgiveness. When applied liberally and regularly, it allows you to handle harsh words with an understanding and nondefensive attitude.

Followers of Jesus are men and women of "no reputation." God should get the glory, and He grants us a good name. Go to the Lord when your pride has been punctured by poisonous words, and ask Him for strength to forgive and grace to extend pleasant words. Don't stew when you have been stung by slander. Rather, apply the ointment of God's grace. Pleasant words work out the hurt and so it will give way to hope. "I love you." "I believe in you." "How can I help?" "How can I pray for you?" Words like these bring out the best in those in need of soul nourishment. Emotions venture back out into vulnerability within a safe environment of encouragement. Offer pleasant words to feed hungry hearts.

"Gracious words are a honeycomb, sweet to the soul and healing to the bones" (Proverbs 16:24).

What pleasant words can I use to mend a wounded relationship?

Related Readings
Proverbs 12:25; 15:4; Zechariah 1:13; Acts 20:2; 1 Peter 5:12

57

Patient Endurance

∞

*This calls for patient endurance and
faithfulness on the part of God's people.*

REVELATION 13:10

Patient endurance is not easy, but it is necessary. If you change jobs every two years, ten times in a row, you do not have twenty years of work experience. You have two years of work experience in ten different places. Make sure to learn what God intends for you to learn where you are before moving on. One of Satan's ploys is to keep you reactive to life rather than proactive, resulting in a shallow faith.

Your faith has the chance to deepen when you stay somewhere for a while, but your faith remains shallow when you run from resistance. Resistance is a faith builder. When life presses against you—even from all sides—you have the opportunity for growth. This is where patient endurance can serve you well. Patient endurance tells you to stay in your marriage "for better or for worse." Patient endurance allows God to change you for the better, and it encourages you to trust Him to do the same for your spouse.

∞

"Consider him who endured such opposition
from sinners, so that you will not grow
weary and lose heart" (Hebrews 12:3).

Patient endurance is illustrated throughout the Bible. Jesus patiently endured the cross. He patiently endured His critics, and ultimately, He more than restored His reputation when He proved His claims by His resurrected life. David patiently endured the fallout from his adultery and murder. He had pushed himself to the point of totally turning his back on God, but instead, he turned back to God and became a broken and humbled leader. Hannah patiently endured her inability to bear children. Her faithfulness to God during barrenness was a testimony of encouragement to friends, family, and a nation. Her womb was empty, but her faith was pregnant with God's possibilities.

Do not confuse procrastination with patient endurance. Patient endurance is active and productive. It is not misguided, apathetic, or irresponsible waiting. It is daily depending on and seeking God for His best. Therefore, patiently endure for God's sake and for the sake of others. Heavenly rewards await those who patiently endure. Use your influence to help others patiently endure their situations. Faithfulness—especially when you don't feel it naturally—is evidence of a maturing faith. You may be on the verge of experiencing God's very best. Patient endurance pays off!

"You have heard of Job's perseverance and have seen
what the Lord finally brought about" (James 5:11).

How can I grow my patience in affliction, so I can be a blessing to those around me for Jesus's sake?

Related Readings
Acts 14:21-22; Romans 5:3; Philippians 1:27-30;
Hebrews 10:32,36; James 1:2-4

58

Call for Wisdom

∞

This calls for wisdom.

REVELATION 13:18

Wisdom is required more often than we realize. Wisdom cuts through emotion and gets to the reality of the situation. "What is the wise thing to do?" is an effective question in decision making. "What is best for the enterprise?" is a wise question to ask as it relates to business and ministry. Many times God speaks through money or the lack thereof. If money is tight, we need to be extremely wise with expenditures. Wisdom tells us to wait for the Lord's provision before spending.

Do you solicit wisdom on a consistent basis? Knowledge and experience mixed with common sense and discernment is a great recipe for wisdom. Wisdom is seeking to understand God's perspective on matters. This is why the wisdom found in God's Word is so relevant for living.

The Bible is a treasure trove waiting to be discovered by the wisdom hunter. Pray, read, and meditate on the Bible, but also seek out the wise. Look for people with gray in their hair, people who exhibit wise behavior. They will help you choose the best course.

∞

"Walk with the wise and become wise, for a
companion of fools suffers harm" (Proverbs 13:20).

Wisdom's crown jewel is the fear of the Lord: "The fear of the LORD is the beginning of knowledge, but fools despise wisdom and discipline" (Proverbs 1:7). The fear of God positions you to receive wisdom. Having no fear of God means you lack wisdom. No wonder our world is filled with fools. We have lost our fear of God, and wisdom has eluded us. The fear of the Lord is an incubator for wisdom, as God dispenses wisdom to those who fear Him.

Love God, worship God, learn from God, serve God…and fear Him. Your fear of God qualifies you for wisdom. Do not become so familiar with God that you lose your fear of God—that would lead to foolishness. Wisdom awaits your humble prayer. Pluck it and enjoy it like plump, luscious fruit on a hot summer day. Taste and see that wisdom is good. No one has ever complained of attaining too much wisdom. Call on wisdom often. Ask God and wise people for wisdom, for this is the faithful thing to do.

———⊗∾———

"If any of you lacks wisdom, you should ask God,
who gives generously to all without finding
fault, and it will be given to you" (James 1:5).

Who are the wise people in my life with whom I can spend time and learn from their experiences?

Related Readings
1 Kings 3:3-15; Proverbs 2:6; Luke 2:52; 1 Corinthians 1:25

59

Praise to God During Pain

∽∞∾

They sang a new song before the throne and
before the four living creatures and the elders.

REVELATION 14:3

As I recovered from cancer treatment a few years ago, I found the physical discomfort to be excruciating. I asked my wife, Rita, for the pain medication. I also asked her to hold me and play the worship song "How He Loves Us." We sat together embracing each other as we praised and worshipped God. One line in the song, which refers to our afflictions being eclipsed by glory, became very real in my painful condition. In the middle of our little worship service, I felt a whole lot of my heavenly Father's love. Praising God amid our pain releases His reassuring refrain: "I love you."

During the intense pain of intimidation, the beast uses fearful manipulation by marking those who bow to his economic threats (Revelation 13:16-18)—but the 144,000 new followers of Jesus learn to sing a new song of praise to their Savior and Lord. Contrary to the beast, these blameless believers are marked by their Father and the Lamb and are compelled to heartfelt worship.

∽∞∾

"As for me, afflicted and in pain—may your salvation,
God, protect me. I will praise God's name in song
and glorify him with thanksgiving" (Psalm 69:29-30).

God's grace gives us the ability to praise and thank Him in the middle of our most severe afflictions. Our praise perspective sees and receives the Lord's love above our adversity. We may have encountered unjust treatment, but we know the Just One is in control. Our Savior Jesus, who allows us to be confined for a time, is the same Savior who sends an earthquake to set us free. When we praise the Lord in our pain, we gain His peace. Hymns sung to God draw us closer to Him.

Our pain may come in many forms: rejection, loneliness, financial stress, guilt over the past, fear of the future, chronic caregiving, marital strife, or a friend who let us down. Ask the Lord to help you be emboldened in your faith, not embittered, as you journey with Jesus through trials. God inhabits the praises of His people (Psalm 22:3). Praise God in your pain, and you will give glory to His fame. Praise sets you free to serve in the Spirit's strength. Pray not to be pain-free, but to be set free.

"The Lord is my strength and my shield; my heart trusts in him, and he helps me. My heart leaps for joy, and with my song I praise him" (Psalm 28:7).

Lord, help me praise You in my pain so that I will gain Your peace and be drawn closer to You.

Related Readings
Psalm 112:7; Isaiah 26:3; Romans 5:3-5; James 1:2-4; 1 Peter 4:13

60

Love Loves the Truth

◦◦◦◦◦

No lie was found in their mouths; they are blameless.

REVELATION 14:5

Truth reveals hidden realities. Hence, the lover of truth daily discovers new opportunities to walk wisely in the ways of Christ. Because He is the Truth, a love relationship with Jesus illuminates truth by His Spirit and illustrates truth by His life. The fruit of truth grows in a life of educated faith. Those who romance truth in God's Word grow to know Him in deeper intimacy. Just as a loving husband pursues his wife, so loving followers of Jesus seek out His truth and His example.

Are your relationships founded on truth or deception? If you commit to open agendas, pure motives, and transparent communication, you value truth. Honesty is a tool for loving correction, not a club for angry retaliation. You speak the truth in love to one another and so bear one another's burdens. You rejoice as you do life together. Speaking the truth encourages trust between people as friends forge a relationship free of dishonesty.

◦◦◦◦◦

"Love does not delight in evil but rejoices
with the truth" (1 Corinthians 13:6).

Love loves the truth. When we love someone enough to lead them from their ignorance, we show we care. Love takes the time to explain and instruct, not complain and erupt. You patiently instruct your children in the teachings of Christ so they will come to know Him and grow in His grace. Even though the whole story can be difficult to tell, help your child to respect the truth.

Season the truth with the spices of humility and grace. Truth is volatile in the hands of a prideful messenger, but embedded in a heart of humble grace, the truth transforms the one who hears it. "Rather, we have renounced secret and shameful ways; we do not use deception, nor do we distort the word of God. On the contrary, by setting forth the truth plainly we commend ourselves to everyone's conscience in the sight of God" (2 Corinthians 4:2). Also, use humor to soften hard facts that seem harsh when spoken directly. Levity can assist you when the seriousness of a situation becomes real. Above all, love Jesus, who is truth personified. His Spirit will direct you to live truth in a spirit of love.

"Dear children, let us not love with words or speech
but with actions and in truth" (1 John 3:18).

Heavenly Father, my heart is to know You and Your truth so I can help others be set free.

Related Readings
Psalm 145:18; Romans 12:9; Ephesians 5:9; 2 John 1-3

61

Shameless Proclamation of the Gospel

*I saw another angel flying in midair, and he had the
eternal gospel to proclaim to those who live on the
earth—to every nation, tribe, language and people.*

REVELATION 14:6

Satan sometimes shames seekers when they begin to take God and His Word seriously. The enemy plants seeds of doubt related to intellectual honesty and the fear of being labeled a religious fanatic. The devil wants Jesus believers to be apologetic and embarrassed to live for the Lord, not declaring His teachings as the gospel truth. But in fact, there is no shame in standing up for Christ and His commands. Faith reveals His fame.

Instead, we are to be ashamed of sin and its deplorable outcome, while embracing wise living. Shame enslaves us in our self-focused behavior, but we are emancipated by our selfless service to others. Our Savior Jesus does not seek to motivate us out of disgrace; rather He infuses His grace into our inner being. The good news of salvation in Christ gives us the confidence to love all people. God's power is shameless.

"If anyone is ashamed of me and my words in this
adulterous and sinful generation, the Son of Man
will be ashamed of them when he comes in his
Father's glory with the holy angels" (Mark 8:38).

Your prayer is for Jesus to be unashamed of you. Offer Him your daily attitude and actions to anoint with His favor. Can your conduct pass the scrutiny of your Savior's examination? Is there anything in your life that could bring reproach to His name? Holy reverence for God avoids any potential embarrassment to His name. Because you deeply respect your heavenly Father, you honor Him with a life that brings Him glory.

His power rests on you when the gospel governs your worldview. The Lord's power exerts itself with quiet but effective influence. God entrusts you with the power of His ideas to do good for Him. Harness the Holy Spirit's energy for eternal purposes. Look for ways to get the gospel to those who are sick, in prison, neglected in nursing homes, and hungry in housing projects. Work to share the good news with every tribe, nation, language, and people. There is no shame in representing your Savior Jesus, so be stunningly shameless.

"I am not ashamed of the gospel, because
it is the power of God that brings salvation
to everyone who believes: first to the Jew,
then to the Gentile" (Romans 1:16).

Lord, how can I be shameless in declaring and living out Your good news?

Related Readings
Genesis 2:25; Psalm 25:3; Isaiah 54:4; Romans 6:21;
Philippians 1:20

62

Resist Ungodly Spiritual Influences

*A third angel followed them and said in a loud voice:
"If anyone worships the beast and its image and
receives its mark on their forehead or on their hand,
they, too, will drink the wine of God's fury, which has
been poured full strength into the cup of his wrath."*

REVELATION 14:9-10

Unholy, unseen forces press their agenda of doubt, lies, and temptation onto God fearers. Unrighteous influences do not rest until they make believers in Jesus restless in their faith. Evil authorities of darkness look for ways to create fear and uncertainty. Demons laugh when they can pit good people against one another. They try to confuse Christians who are stuck in a spiritual struggle.

The beast is an unholy force that attempts to force his mark of loyalty on those who reject God. The Lord is our holy advocate who defeats unholy spiritual forces. Yes, Jesus has broken the devil's power over life and death. Like a roaring lion, Satan still tries to intimidate and manipulate us into a fearful panic, but Christ is King. He has tamed the toothless tyrant. Our Savior is with us as we struggle.

———

*"Do not turn to mediums or seek out
spiritists, for you will be defiled by them. I
am the LORD your God" (Leviticus 19:31).*

As you search for spiritual reality and stability, avoid false teachers and spiritists who call up the dead—for they are dead wrong. The occult, astrologists, and horoscopes are a spiritual sham that only feed fanciful living. Your heart hungers for help, but you are wise to protect it from spiritual junk food. Satisfy your soul's appetite with healthy routines. Engage in a Bible-believing church, meditate daily on Scripture, pray, and meet regularly in a caring community of Christians.

If you struggle alone in your spiritual quest, you will miss God's best. However, when you have a safe environment to share with other struggling saints, you will see Jesus in them. The Holy Spirit works through other submitted followers of God to give you comfort when you are hurting and wisdom when you are unsure. Like a good soldier, surround yourself with a squad of loyal comrades who watch your back. Prayers of righteous friends frustrate the devil and his demons. Your struggles will subside as you feel peace from prayer support and when your hope is in Christ!

"Our struggle is not against flesh and blood, but against the rulers, against the authorities, against the powers of this dark world and against the spiritual forces of evil in the heavenly realms" (Ephesians 6:12).

Heavenly Father, I need You to stabilize my faith as I struggle with doubt and confusion.

Related Readings
Leviticus 20:6; Isaiah 8:19; John 20:27; Romans 8:37-39

63

Remain Faithful

⬿⬿⬿

Remain faithful to Jesus.

REVELATION 14:12

Faithfulness tends to be practiced by the few. However, for all committed followers of Christ, the clarion call is to remain faithful. He is the object of your adoration and your obedience, and He deserves and desires your faithfulness. It should be easier to remain faithful when the object of your faithfulness is as pure as the driven snow. There is nothing about Jesus that doesn't elicit faithfulness. His fairness invites faithfulness; His grace and generosity generate faithfulness; His love longs for faithfulness; His holiness inspires faithfulness; His compassion creates faithfulness; His forgiveness foretells faithfulness; His judgment motivates faithfulness; His life models faithfulness. Jesus remained faithful to the very end, and in Him, so can you.

Is there anything about Jesus that keeps you from remaining faithful? Who else can you go to for eternal life (John 6:68)? Faithfulness to Jesus is par for the Christian life. He is the standard by which you live. Even under the onslaught of illness, remain faithful. As circumstances around you crumble, remain faithful. When people mistreat and misunderstand you, remain faithful. If you lose your job, remain faithful. When a close friend lets you down and rejects you, remain faithful. Faithfulness to Jesus is the chorus of Christian living.

⬿⬿⬿

"I have sent to you Timothy, my son whom I love,

who is faithful in the Lord. He will remind you of my
way of life in Christ Jesus" (1 Corinthians 4:17).

His faithfulness to you is the measure of your capacity to remain faithful. The indwelling of the Holy Spirit provides you with the capability to remain faithful. Remaining faithful to people is a natural byproduct of remaining faithful to Jesus, and your faithfulness may be the very thing that draws them to Him. Faithfulness reminds people of a faithful Savior who loves and forgives.

Make it a goal to remain faithful to "undeserving" relatives or friends. Your attitude toward them may attract them to God. You may need to dissolve a working partnership, but you can still salvage the relationship. You can remain faithful even when the other party doesn't. Let your faithfulness, not your feelings, be the gauge for your giving, your service, your forgiveness, and your love. Above all else, remain faithful to Jesus, for He is the Faithful One.

—⁕—

"He is the Maker of heaven and earth, the
sea, and everything in them—he remains
faithful forever" (Psalm 146:6).

Who needs me to remain faithful to our relationship, even though they have been unfaithful?

Related Readings
Micah 7:2; 2 Timothy 2:13; Hebrews 8:9; Revelation 2:13

64

Reward of Faithfulness

⚬⚬⚬

*This calls for patient endurance on the
part of the people of God who keep his
commands and remain faithful to Jesus.*

REVELATION 14:12

Faithfulness is doing what I said I would do. It is an integrity issue. Commitments are not to be taken lightly. For example, a verbal commitment is an unwritten contract. However, these can be the most risky and the most misunderstood. If we make a verbal commitment, it behooves us to make sure it is plain with all parties involved. Slow down, communicate more, and show up on time for appointments. Less is more. Most of us would be much better off if we made fewer commitments.

The Lord has been faithful even in our unfaithfulness. God does what He says He will. He is faithful to forgive our sin, and He leads us to forgive too. He is faithful to convict us of sin and to lead us into righteousness. He is faithful to flood our souls with peace, joy, and contentment. God understands what it means to keep a commitment—even at great cost. The death of His only Son was the fulfillment of an old promise. Indeed, the Lord is faithful to the faithful.

⚬⚬⚬

"To the faithful you show yourself faithful, to the
blameless you show yourself blameless" (Psalm 18:25).

After conversion, we commit to following Christ. Following Jesus requires fidelity of faith. There are no equals to our love for Him. He tells us in His Word to "let our yes be yes and our no be no," and we obey because we want to be faithful to Him and others.

Unfaithfulness will catch up with us. How many of us go to bed with conflicting relational commitments? Do not let work, hobbies, children, or money become your idols of activity. Faithfulness begins and ends with follow-through with our commitments to God.

Yes, the Lord rewards your faithfulness. Your faithfulness does not go unnoticed. One of the greatest rewards is the gift of trust. Faithfulness births trust and grows trust, so over time you earn the reputation of a trustworthy person. Those who can be trusted with a little can be trusted with much. Thus, be faithful, so you can be trusted. Above all, be faithful because He is faithful. A faithful servant will hear their Master Jesus say, "Well done!"

—✳—

"His master replied, 'Well done, good and faithful
servant! You have been faithful with a few things; I
will put you in charge of many things. Come and
share your master's happiness!'" (Matthew 25:23).

How is the Lord faithful to me? To what commitment do I need to remain faithful?

Related Readings
Deuteronomy 7:9; 11:13-15; Psalm 37:28; Matthew 5:37;
1 Timothy 1:12

65

Finish Well

~~~

I heard a voice from heaven say, "Write this: Blessed
are the dead who die in the Lord from now on."
REVELATION 14:13

God is not looking for perfection, but He does desire passion for Himself and obedience to His Word. People who do not finish well have decided to take control themselves. They act as if they have a better plan than God. This type of decision-making process will have limited success, if any, in the Lord's eyes. Does it mean we will have no regrets when we finish well? No.

The Christian life is a marathon. Jesus is at the finish line, and as you run, you are surrounded by an eternal entourage of people who have been faithful before. Your Savior and His saints are praying for you and encouraging you to finish well—which is His will. Don't lose heart or become proud. Keep your focus on the ultimate destination: the prize of Christ's commendation that awaits you. Die in the Lord and you will live eternally with the Lord.

~~~

"Therefore, since we are surrounded by such a great
cloud of witnesses, let us throw off everything that
hinders and the sin that so easily entangles. And let
us run with perseverance the race marked out for us,
fixing our eyes on Jesus, the pioneer and perfecter of
faith. For the joy set before him he endured the cross,

> scorning its shame, and sat down at the right hand
> of the throne of God. Consider him who endured
> such opposition from sinners, so that you will not
> grow weary and lose heart" (Hebrews 12:1-3).

Along the race of life you will encounter difficulty. You will tire and need rest. You will have lonely stretches of road where you feel like quitting. At other times the race will seem like an uphill battle, with every muscle in your body screaming for attention. But thankfully, there are times of refreshment and rejuvenation. After you have run up a hill of hope, there is an opportunity to enjoy the righteous run down the other side. Intimacy with God positions you to hear His voice, obey Him, and finish well.

Finishing well means you live as if you are dying—because we all are terminal. We must live today for Christ, since tomorrow may not come. We live best when we live as if today were our last day. Finish well today on behalf of your heavenly Father, family, and friends. A life well spent makes your Savior smile and say...

—— ⤬ ——

"Well done, my good servant!" (Luke 19:17).

What does it mean for me to finish well? Am I finishing well today?

Related Readings
Proverbs 20:28; Isaiah 26:2; Acts 27:25; 2 Timothy 4:6-8

66

Rest from Work

---

*"Yes," says the Spirit, "they will rest from their
labor, for their deeds will follow them."*

REVELATION 14:13

Some people have a hard time resting from their work. They love their work, enjoy their work, and may even worship their work. Hard, smart, and productive work is good, but worshipping work is bad. Doing so is reckless and can lead to ruin in our relationships, our bodies, and even our finances. Work that is worshipped gets out of hand quickly. God is the only one who deserves worship. It is good to be proud of quality work, but do not allow work to become an end in itself. Your true identity comes from Christ, not work.

When you work all the time, your moorings of faith tend to drift from Christ to yourself. "Can God be trusted enough for me to rest from my work?" Of course—He divinely redeems the time of your limited work and produces lasting results. You are His workmanship in Christ Jesus; when you take the time to cease working, God accelerates His work in you. Some of His best work takes place when you are resting from your labor. Believers rest for eternity, while unbelievers are in torment forever.

"There remains, then, a Sabbath-rest for the
people of God; for anyone who enters God's

> rest also rests from his own works, just as
> God did from His" (Hebrews 4:9-10).

You can physically be away from work and still be at work mentally, so free your mind from this split-focused activity. Do not make your mind jealous over your body's freedom from work. Rest your thoughts from work, and you will discover your thinking is more robust and innovative when you reengage. Shift your thinking to the bigger thoughts of God and His plan. Superimpose simple faith in Him over the complex issues that are assaulting your rest.

Your mind, body, and emotions are all part of your Sabbath rest. Your Sabbath rest can be a catalyst for others to engage God. Set the example and watch others follow. Your Sabbath rest gives others permission to do the same. It's not always easy to get to God's rest, but once you arrive, it is well worth the effort. His rest ignites your obedience and trust, so rest from work and rest in Him. Then watch your work become better, more productive—sustained by the Spirit.

> "Let us, therefore, make every effort to enter that
> rest, so that no one will perish by following their
> example of disobedience" (Hebrews 4:11).

What areas of my life do I need to leave in the Lord's hands?

Related Readings
Psalms 46:10; 62:1-8; Galatians 1:10; Hebrews 4:1;
Revelation 14:13

67

Harvest of Unholiness

<hr>

The angel swung his sickle on the earth,
gathered its grapes and threw them into
the great winepress of God's wrath.

REVELATION 14:19

The promise of eternal judgment and hell is not fun to talk about, but the somber reality is relayed by our Savior Jesus. He is our Savior because He saves us from our sins and from eternal damnation in hell. Hell brings separation, but Jesus brings reconciliation. Hell brings torment, but Jesus brings peace. Hell brings darkness, but Jesus brings light. Hell hurts, but heaven heals.

The same loving Lord who promises heaven also promises hell. Indeed, heaven is sweeter because of the sour taste eternal separation from God leaves on the lips. We begin our experience of hell on earth when we choose our own way instead of Christ's way. Separation from God here on earth is a precursor to separation from the Almighty in eternity. Hell is a fearful place of loneliness that lacks love and security. An angel from heaven will swing his sickle of judgment on earth, harvesting unholy grapes—evildoers destined for God's winepress of wrath.

<hr>

"I will show you whom you should fear: Fear him who,
after your body has been killed, has authority to throw
you into hell. Yes, I tell you, fear him" (Luke 12:5).

The fear of the Lord brings focus to His holiness and our unholy condition outside of Christ. You may experience the wrath of men because you choose to fear God, but better to be known as a God-fearing man or woman than to experience the wrath of God. The power of man looks powerless in the presence of the One who has the power to cast the unsaved into hell. Sinners in the hands of a holy God desperately need His grace.

You and I are blessed to have the opportunity to believe in Jesus Christ as the Son of the living God. He saves us not only from hell but also from our sins and from ourselves. By His sacrificial love, He exchanges eternity in an unrighteous hell for a righteous heaven. Yes, you can repent on your deathbed, but why not start heaven's journey now? Hell's fury is for the faithless, but when you walk by faith, you have only the Lord to fear.

✺

"Therefore, there is now no condemnation for those who are in Christ Jesus, because through Christ Jesus the law of the Spirit who gives life has set you free from the law of sin and death" (Romans 8:1-2).

Lord, give me holy boldness and uncommon compassion to warn the unholy of Your wrath to come.

Related Readings
Matthew 23:33; Mark 9:43-47; Luke 16:22-24; James 3:6; 2 Peter 2:4-9

68

Songs of Deliverance

⸺⸙⸺

*They held harps given them by God and sang the
song of God's servant Moses and of the Lamb: "Great
and marvelous are your deeds, Lord God Almighty.
Just and true are your ways, King of the nations."*

REVELATION 15:2-3

As followers of Jesus, we can sing a song of deliverance—for the Lord has liberated us by His love, freed us from fear, and adopted us as His beloved children!

John describes with striking imagery the defeated beast, who represents our fleshly desires. The Lamb defeated our foe with His sacrifice on the cross. Ultimately, we who worship the Lamb will celebrate at the seashore of our salvation—our final deliverance over the beast. We will sing the song of Moses, with lyrics from the Lord who freed His children from the bondage of their own beast—Pharaoh. The Red Sea swallowed up the Egyptian army. Any adversaries of Almighty God are destined to defeat. We worship here, anticipating our victory party there!

⸺⸙⸺

"Then Moses and the Israelites sang this song
to the LORD: 'I will sing to the LORD, for he
is highly exalted. Both horse and driver he
has hurled into the sea" (Exodus 15:1).

Do you ever feel as though you are a slave to a nagging sin—one that won't let you go? Shame may keep you chained inside a self-made solitary confinement. Love bids you to come out of sin's shadow and enjoy the Lord's light of complete and total acceptance. Resist feeling unworthy by remembering with joyful thanksgiving that a worthy Lamb was slain for your sin and reigns as King of the ages. Christ is a Christian's only Master. A slave to Jesus is mastered by Him.

Since we have been saved from sin, we sing grateful anthems, including "Amazing Grace": "The Lord has promised good to me. His word my hope secures; He will my shield and portion be as long as life endures." Like a melodious, orange-breasted robin, a soul that's been set free flees from its fears and flies almost effortlessly upon the wind of invisible love. Sing, yes, sing! The Holy Spirit delivers you out of sin into your Savior's love.

"My lips will shout for joy when I sing praise to you—I whom you have delivered. My tongue will tell of your righteous acts all day long, for those who wanted to harm me have been put to shame and confusion" (Psalm 71:23-24).

What nagging sin has the Lord delivered me from that causes me to shout praise and thanksgiving?

Related Readings

2 Samuel 22:1-4; Psalms 20:5; 144:9; Isaiah 12:5; Ephesians 5:19

69

Fear of the Lord

―――――∞∞∞―――――

*Who will not fear you, Lord, and bring glory
to your name? For you alone are holy.*

REVELATION 15:4

I had two types of high school football coaches. I was afraid of one
coach because of his tirades and his angry, intimidating language.
He motivated me for a short time because I was afraid of not doing
precisely what he wanted. The second coach also expected a high standard of performance, but he was both instructional and inspirational.
I knew I had room for failure with him, but my goal was growth. I per-
ceived the first coach as an angry man who expected perfection. Of
course, I could never please him. The second coach simply expected
my best—and he got it. As a result, he and I could celebrate together.

The fear of the Lord is the foundation of wisdom. Without awe
of the Almighty, we have no access to His insight. When we lack reverence for His holiness, we also lack an understanding of God's ways.
The first step in acquiring wisdom from Almighty God is to fear Him
(Proverbs 9:10). Reverence includes worshipping the Lord's majesty
and dreading His judgment. Once we embrace a healthy fear of the
Lord, we discover peace, knowledge, and love for the Holy One.

―――――∞∞∞―――――

"Praise the LORD! How joyful are those
who fear the LORD and delight in obeying
his commands" (Psalm 112:1 NLT).

If you are driven by guilt or shame or feel the need for perfect behavior to be accepted by God, you will always believe that you fall short and that the Lord is not pleased with you. But if you see your heavenly Father's love and holiness as a refuge in a world of chaos and confusion, you will learn to rest in Christ and learn from Him. You fear God by fearing the consequences of sin, but you freely receive His forgiveness when you do sin. Fear of the Lord draws you closer to Him.

The fear of God is the pathway to freely worshipping and praising Him. Those who have experienced salvation in Jesus—who have been rescued from the wrath of the Almighty—have a holy cheerfulness they lift to the Lord in gratitude and thankful praise. Joy in Jesus is the language of heartfelt worship. The more we fear the Lord's holiness, the more we are free to love and worship Him for who He is—our heavenly Father, the Maker of heaven and earth. Hell has neither fury nor flames of fear for those who fear God alone!

"Serve the LORD with reverent fear, and rejoice with trembling" (Psalm 2:11 NLT).

What does it mean for me to fear God but not be afraid of God?

Related Readings
Nehemiah 1:11; Psalm 96:9; Proverbs 14:26; 19:23; Revelation 14:7

70

Covenant of Love

~∞~

After this I looked, and I saw in heaven the temple—that is,
the tabernacle of the covenant law—and it was opened.

REVELATION 15:5

The Lord's covenant law is completed by His covenant of love with Israel and His covenant of love with His church, the bride of Christ. We are united with Christ in the bonds of love forever. Yes, those who fall in love with Jesus stand at the altar of trust and vow to remain faithful until death brings them into eternal oneness with their Lord. Our fidelity is evidence of our genuine love and commitment to God. His covenant of love compels us to be loved and to love.

God loves us unconditionally, even when we fail to reciprocate His love. Though the Lord's love is jealous, He does not jettison us from His presence when we ignore Him. We may drift away from Him with our unwise decisions, but His love is available to bring us back to the security and serenity of His presence. Christ's covenant of love to His forgiven bride keeps us humble and grateful. Because of His great love for us, we long to love and obey the Lord Jesus.

~∞~

"LORD, the God of heaven, the great and awesome God
…keeps his covenant of love with those who love him
and keep his commandments" (Nehemiah 1:5).

We love the Lord because He first loved us. We pursue the Lord because He first pursued us. We serve the Lord because He first served us. We remain faithful to the Lord because He remains faithful to us. Yes, we love Him and keep His commands because of what His grace and love have already done for us. His is a divine gift that provides what we need most. Our greatest need is to be loved by our heavenly Father. Christ's covenant of love grows love in our own hearts.

God's covenant of love is not to be taken for granted. It should not be an emotional acknowledgment we act on only when our feelings cooperate. No, when we entered into covenant with Christ, we committed to Christ and to all He represents: love, obedience, generosity, holiness, service, worship, prayer, Scripture, mercy, grace, forgiveness, evangelism, discipleship, and the church. Since He keeps His covenant of love, we are the bride of Christ who loves, cherishes, and obeys.

"We know and rely on the love God has for
us. God is love. Whoever lives in love lives
in God, and God in them" (1 John 4:16).

Heavenly Father, thank You for Your covenant of love, which invites me to be loved by You and compels me to love You and others.

Related Readings
Daniel 9:4; Matthew 22:37-40; 1 Corinthians 13:13; 16:14; Galatians 5:6; 1 John 4:7-12

71

Benefits of Repentance

They refused to repent and glorify him.
REVELATION 16:9

Authentic repentance is not perfunctory, but fruitful in its follow-through. When the Holy Spirit arrests my heart and pricks my conscience about my behavior, I want to change. A bold, loving friend may expose my bad habit or unacceptable attitude. If so, will I change? Indeed, fruitful repentance is not only words of remorse, but also a change in the way I have been acting. Repentance is the removal of my pride, an encounter with my blind spots.

Fruitful repentance may be the hardest for those of us who have been in the faith for a long time. We get settled into a mode of thinking that quits learning and growing. We can become comfortable with Christ and forget to fear Him. We can take God for granted and go places with our mind that a newfound faith would have forbidden. Make certain that excuses or cover-ups do not become default actions when you encounter a need for change. Pride refuses to repent, be fruitful, or glorify God.

"Produce fruit in keeping with
repentance" (Matthew 3:8).

When you hear truth that is contrary to your living, how do you respond? If you have a secret between you and God, it will get worse unless you confess it to others. Do not hide behind your teaching role in the church or your status with your family. People who love you will love you more when you come clean about your judgmental attitude, a flirtatious relationship, or an air of spiritual superiority. For example, don't hide any spending from your husband or wife, as this leads to great loss of trust between spouses. Penitent people do not conceal their sin—they reveal it.

So what are some evidences of fruitful repentance? "The fruit of the Spirit is love, joy, peace, forbearance, kindness, goodness, faithfulness, gentleness and self-control" (Galatians 5:22-23). Real repentance is not just embarrassment over being caught, but also taking responsibility with positive and proactive changes for the good. There is a transformation from haughtiness to humility, judgment to grace, fear to trust, and pride to penitence. Truly repentant people fear the Lord and find rest for their souls as they return to good standing.

———— ✸ ————

"This is what the Sovereign LORD, the Holy One of Israel, says: 'In repentance and rest is your salvation, in quietness and trust is your strength, but you would have none of it'" (Isaiah 30:15).

What attitude or actions of mine do I need to change? What positive fruit in my life is evidence of my repentance?

Related Readings
2 Chronicles 32:26; Psalm 51:1-13; Matthew 21:32; Acts 3:19

72

Why Some Curse God

*They cursed God on account of the plague of
hail, because the plague was so terrible.*

REVELATION 16:21

God does not waste pain. Jesus came to defeat the enemy by way of suffering on the cross, not by way of inflicting violence on the violent. Man's violent act toward Christ turned into God's extravagant love and forgiveness through Jesus. My heart hurts when I see pictures of innocent victims whose bloody bodies are riddled by bullets or bombs from cowardly terrorists. My sense of justice is outraged. Where is God amid these ungodly acts? What should be our response to suffering?

Some curse God because they do not see God in their circumstances—He feels foreign and disinterested in their desperate situation. But it is in our feelings of desperation that we desperately need the Lord. He calls us to praise Him, not curse Him when our pain is the most intense. Unbelievers curse God for His judgment, while believers praise God for His matchless mercy.

"It only makes sense that God, by whom and
for whom everything exists, would choose to
bring many of us to His side by using suffering
to perfect Jesus, the founder of our faith, the
pioneer of our salvation" (Hebrews 2:10 VOICE).

Does your suffering or someone else's seem unfair or unnecessary? If so, by faith seek to see the bigger story of Christ's salvation at work in other needy souls. Our Lord Jesus does not waste pain. Just as modern technology generates electricity from recycled landfill waste, so God's amazing grace can rescue souls buried in a landfill of lost love. Instead of seeing injustice as just another needless crime, the Holy Spirit uses injustice to justify those separated from God in their sin. Your long-suffering is the Spirit's opportunity to draw lost souls to Jesus.

So, what does the Lord expect of us in the middle of suffering? Our heavenly Father's desire is for His children to draw deeper into Christ's living water from His well of grace. Satan may try to ambush our trust in Jesus with trials and tribulations, or even worse, fame and fortune. But though our bodies and souls may suffer, we gladly endure pain for the sake of the gospel. Suffering is the canvas on which Christ etches His eternal invitation to be with Him.

"I want to know Christ—yes, to know the power of his resurrection and participation in his sufferings" (Philippians 3:10).

Who needs my comfort and prayers in the middle of current pain and suffering?

Related Readings
Zephaniah 3:19-20; Luke 24:26; 2 Corinthians 1:6; 1 Thessalonians 5:9; Hebrews 5:8

73

Spiritual Prostitution

∞

The name written on her forehead was a mystery:
Babylon the great, the mother of prostitutes
and of the abominations of the earth.

REVELATION 17:5

Unfortunately, there are those who use religion to get their way. Unseemly businesspeople use the art of Christian conversation to give the appearance of having values and principles based on the Bible. However, once they make the sale or close the deal, their self-serving and dishonest ways reveal who they really are—promoters of false spirituality. Some single adults may even prey on other unsuspecting single adults in church. They attend church to form relationships and then take advantage of trusting souls.

One of the worst types of deception is spiritual deception—using God to get our way. In marriage a husband may use submission to control his wife, or a wife may use grace to withhold physical intimacy from her husband. Therefore, warn those who try to buy the Holy Spirit for their benefit, like Simon in the early church (Acts 8:17-19). Instead, we cultivate authentic spirituality in our hearts and minds through prayer, worship, and community. Those who use religion to satisfy sensual desires will one day be exposed as imposters.

∞

"She took hold of him and kissed him and
with a brazen face she said: 'Today I fulfilled

my vows, and I have food from my fellowship
offering at home'" (Proverbs 7:13-14).

True spirituality, on the other hand, is motivated and controlled by
the Spirit of Christ. Almighty God initiates authentic faith. True spirituality does not only look out for itself but is sincerely concerned with
serving others. You are comfortable in the presence of authentic believers because you know they care for you. Their business and religious
activities are signposts of their integrity.

Their yes is their yes, and their no is their no. What you see is
what you get. True spirituality comes over time—forged on the anvil
of adversity, taught at the hearth of humility, and received at the gate
of God's grace. You know your religion is real when you love others
above your own needs and you care for the poor and needy. True spirituality leads others to love God and obey His commands—unstained
by the ways of the world.

———⟨∞⟩———

"Pure and undefiled religion in the sight of our
God and Father is this: to visit orphans and
widows in their distress, and to keep oneself
unstained by the world" (James 1:27 NASB).

Whom do I need to confront in love about using their
"Christianity" for selfish intentions?

Related Readings
Ecclesiastes 7:4; Matthew 25:36; 2 Corinthians 1:17;
Colossians 2:23

74

Wise Decision Making

⸺∞⸺

This calls for a mind with wisdom.

REVELATION 17:9

Wise decision making is not accidental, but intentional. A wise person has a humble understanding of the need for the Lord's insightful solutions to very serious issues. Wisdom comes over time to those whose priority is wisdom hunting. Like a patient hunter who looks for the best time and place to bag game, so seekers of wisdom are always in search of scriptural trophies of truth.

Humble seekers will find wisdom. Wise decision making is necessary in a life that leverages the Lord's favor. The Almighty is on the lookout for those who align themselves with His agenda. He is wisdom, He offers wisdom, and He blesses wisdom. Wise are we to daily look toward God for His game plan. We especially need wisdom when we have conflicting conclusions to consider. Are you facing a life-or-death dilemma? If so, ask Jesus to show you the wise path to take.

⸺∞⸺

"The wisdom that comes from heaven is first
of all pure; then peace-loving, considerate,
submissive, full of mercy and good fruit,
impartial and sincere" (James 3:17-18).

What if someone makes a decision without consulting you, even though the decision affects your life? Will you decide to respond in humble confrontation or drift away as a victim? Sometimes parents, bosses, or friends make unwise decisions that affect you negatively. Whatever your circumstances, you can find wisdom to work through your turmoil. Or, if you are facing unforeseen success, Holy Scripture can give you insight about excellent financial stewardship.

We make the best decisions when we focus on the long term rather than the short term. Hence, make sure to submit any of your fears to faith. When we ask God for help, generosity overcomes greed and gratitude overcomes discontentment. Impulsiveness gives way to patience. He calms our anxieties and sheds light on the right decisions, the right paths. Are the choices you face today focused exclusively on your needs, or are you motivated by something much bigger than yourself? Seek the Lord for clarity, and confusion will melt away.

⁓⁓⁓

"If any of you lacks wisdom, you should ask God,
who gives generously to all without finding
fault, and it will be given to you" (James 1:5).

God, will You remind me to consult You before I make important decisions?

Related Readings
1 Kings 3:9,16-28; Daniel 1:17; Matthew 7:7; James 3:13

75

God's Purpose Accomplished

———— ∞∞∞ ————

God has put it into their hearts to accomplish his
purpose by agreeing to hand over to the beast their
royal authority, until God's words are fulfilled.

REVELATION 17:17

God will accomplish His purpose. It may be with or without us, but He will execute His will. God does not back down or hold back when it comes to fulfilling His plan. He knows what is best and is bent toward carrying out His good will. Nothing can stop God from accomplishing His purpose. War cannot stop His purpose because He will draw people to Himself amid the atrocities of battle. Illness cannot stop His purpose because He will reveal His care, compassion, and healing. Death cannot stop His purpose because God will graduate believers in Christ to heaven and nonbelievers to hell.

Sin cannot stop His purpose because Christ forgave sin by His death on the cross. Sinners cannot stop His purpose because there are consequences for wrong and, ultimately, judgment by God. Satan cannot stop God's purpose because what the devil means for evil, God can use for good. God's purpose is a freight train that travels down the tracks of obedience and disobedience, saints and sinners. Its momentum on behalf of mankind cannot be stopped. He will not be denied.

———— ∞∞∞ ————

"I have brought you glory on earth by finishing
the work you gave me to do" (John 17:4).

What is God's purpose? One purpose of God is to adopt everyone into His family who believes Jesus is His Son. "For God so loved the world that he gave his one and only Son, that whoever believes in him shall not perish but have eternal life" (John 3:16). Anyone who calls on the name of the Lord will be saved, and this accomplishes one of God's greater purposes.

Are you contributing to the greater heavenly mosaic of God's glorification? Your fulfillment of God's purpose helps others do the same. Therefore, stay laser-focused on executing God's purpose. Pray about it and seek the Scripture to better understand God's purpose for you. Equity in eternity never diminishes, so invest a lot—and invest early. His purpose will be accomplished. Find out where He is working, and join Him to fulfill His mission.

———⊗⊗⊗———

"We know that in all things God works for the good of those who love him, who have been called according to his purpose" (Romans 8:28).

What greater purpose is God calling me to carry out in Jesus's name?

Related Readings
Exodus 9:16; Job 42:2; Acts 13:36; Philippians 2:13

76

Places of Refuge

*I heard another voice from heaven say: "'Come out
of her, my people,' so that you will not share in her
sins, so that you will not receive any of her plagues."*

REVELATION 18:4

My soul can easily go to places that lack real peace, protection, and refreshment. Worry lures me in, especially when I feel financial pressure at work or home. What if I lose my job? What if my friend doesn't understand? What if my health fails and I can't work long enough to care for my family? Like a confused dog, I chase my tail in circles with worry, and the outcome is dizziness and confusion. Worry is a weak refuge, but when I trust in God, I'm reminded that worry is a waste of time. He is the strong tower who casts shadows over our fears.

Self-reliance is another lure when times are hard. My soul resorts to hiding behind my hard work and determination rather than depending on my heavenly Father. Amid my frantic pace, I forget to go to God for His rest, wisdom, and resources. Unless I fight for an unhurried rhythm of work, I run right past my ever-present help—my heavenly Father. My energy alone leaves me exhausted and lonely, but the Lord's refuge replenishes and revives me.

"God is our refuge and strength, an
ever-present help in trouble" (Psalm 46:1).

Self-pity feels good in the moment, but it becomes an incubator for anger. We get mad and say to ourselves, "If only other people would see things my way, the world would be a much better place." We feel sorry for ourselves because we believe no one really understands us. We are wise to remember it's not about us, but God. Our refuge is in Him.

How is your soul? Does it feel like a hash-brown potato—scattered, smothered, or covered? Scattered because so many people are pulling on you? Smothered by your own unrealistic expectations? Or covered by Christ? Fortunately, in each moment of the day—no matter how loud and loony—by faith we can create a sanctuary for our soul. Close the office or bathroom door and close your eyes. Then look to the Lord in prayer. If you can take a walk, step outside, walk with our Savior, and be empowered by His presence. God's refuge is always near.

⸺⸱⸺

> "I will say of the LORD, 'He is my refuge and my fortress, my God, in whom I trust'" (Psalm 91:2).

How can I, by faith, create a sanctuary for my soul to find rest and refuge in God?

Related Readings
Psalm 142:5; Isaiah 33:16; Jeremiah 16:19; Lamentations 3:57; Nahum 1:7

77

Economic Storms

The merchants of the earth will weep and mourn over her because no one buys their cargoes anymore.

REVELATION 18:11

Economic storms expose evil. When the ocean tide goes out, you are able to see what was previously underwater. Dead wood is swept away, never to be seen again. It may seem as though the wicked are prospering, but eventually they will be found out. The Holy Spirit shakes out sin so it can be seen and judged. As the Lord promised His children in the past, "I will shake the people of Israel…as grain is shaken in a sieve" (Amos 9:9). John describes a future worldwide economic meltdown where businesspeople stress out and panic, because there is no one to purchase their products and services.

Is your work based on godly principles that work to bring glory to Him and seek to serve others? Economic storms collapse businesses and ministries that are dependent on debt. Pride is purged when entities collapse, and all manner of excess is exposed. What really matters in life becomes the priority: faith, family, friends, food, and shelter. Storms reveal a shaky foundation of faithlessness or a solid foundation of faith.

"When the storm has swept by, the wicked are gone, but the righteous stand firm forever" (Proverbs 10:25).

Moreover, those who cling to Christ are not shaken. He is our cornerstone, which no degree of chaos can challenge. The righteous cannot be moved because their Master is immovable. Therefore, stand firm in the Lord. "Those who trust in the LORD are like Mount Zion, which cannot be shaken but endures forever" (Psalm 125:1).

Worldly wisdom has a way of reducing heaven's wisdom to an afterthought. After using our worldly wisdom, we pray and try to discern the Lord's ways—but only after our ways do not work. It is tempting to rely on what seems to work instead of asking what principles to live by based on God's economy.

Furthermore, your stability in your Savior is security for your family, friends, and work associates. Your unwavering faith during difficult days offers them peace, encouragement, and conviction. Indeed, if all you have left is a firm foundation of faith, begin rebuilding God's big vision. Are you a wise builder who perseveres through downturns or a foolish opportunist who is swept away by suffering?

<hr />

"Therefore everyone who hears these words of
mine and puts them into practice is like a wise man
who built his house on the rock" (Matthew 7:24).

How can I build my life, home, and work on the solid rock of Jesus?

Related Readings
Job 20:5; Psalm 37:10; Acts 2:25; Hebrews 12:28

78

Uncertainty of Wealth

In one hour such great wealth has been brought to ruin!

REVELATION 18:17

Command those who are rich in this present world not to be arrogant nor to put their hope in wealth, which is so uncertain, but to put their hope in God, who richly provides us with everything for our enjoyment.

1 TIMOTHY 6:17

If one thing is certain, it is the uncertainty of wealth. Riches can fluctuate like a terrifying roller coaster ride. My financial net worth could evaporate overnight, or it could incrementally deteriorate over time. Hope in wealth guarantees you sleepless nights and emotional fatigue. Why would I place my hope in money that migrates all over the map of life? Hope in money leads to false security and creates discontentment.

Yes, it is embarrassing to lose anything, especially money—but it can be replaced. Financial purging peels back our true intent and exposes the object of our affections. Do we love money, or do we love God? We can't love both. Fortunately, hope in heaven is most certain. Christ is our reliable compass during a cash crisis. Jesus's utmost desire is for you to toil for true riches.

"So if you have not been trustworthy in handling worldly wealth, who will trust you with true riches?" (Luke 16:11).

True riches are contentment, trust in God, and generosity. Your passionate pursuit of true riches trumps worries over worldly wealth. Do your children and friends see you lamenting in prayer over the lost souls of men rather than the loss of money? What is the value of one person finding Jesus in a personal and growing relationship? Heavenly wealth compounds eternally with certain rewards, while worldly wealth depreciates and is destroyed.

Therefore, take this time of financial transition and place your affections and certainty in Christ (Colossians 3:1-4). Gently remind the fearful that fear of God and loving people are true riches. Money comes and goes, but Jesus remains faithful. Hope in Christ, not cash, brings contentment and the enjoyment of true wealth. You can be certain of this! No one regrets being generous in the moment, but sad are those who wait to give aggressively, only to experience the evaporation of their net worth. We can ever depend on our generous Savior Jesus!

"Cast but a glance at riches, and they are
gone, for they will surely sprout wings and fly
off to the sky like an eagle" (Proverbs 23:5).

Where can I give a generous financial gift in order to cultivate my certain hope in heaven?

Related Readings
Psalm 42:5; Proverbs 3:9; Matthew 10:42; John 17:8

79

Value Church

Let us rejoice and be glad and give him glory!
For the wedding of the Lamb has come, and
his bride has made herself ready.

REVELATION 19:7

Why do we value church? We value church because God values church. The imagery He uses to illustrate its importance is stunning. It is the picture of a pure and prepared people approaching the Lord, as a bride ready to be received by her husband. The bride of Christ is the church, honored and loved deeply by Jesus. The church is made up of imperfect people, but Jesus will one day make His bride perfect "to present her to himself as a radiant church, without stain or wrinkle or any other blemish, but holy and blameless" (Ephesians 5:27).

You may say, "I don't need the church," but to say this is also to say, "I don't value Jesus's relationships." We automatically care for the spouse of a friend because we honor our friends' relationships. In the same way, Christians who love the Lord also love His bride. Furthermore, we need the church's prayers, accountability, community, fellowship, friendships, teaching, and worship. Pride compels us to resist the church, but humility prompts us to engage with God's people. Investing time and money in the church is investing in eternal rewards.

"Let us consider how we may spur one another on
toward love and good deeds, not giving up meeting

together, as some are in the habit of doing, but
encouraging one another—and all the more as you
see the Day approaching" (Hebrews 10:24-25).

The church needs you to engage enthusiastically. The community of God needs your wisdom, your mentoring, your energy, your Bible knowledge, your experience, your service, your financial gifts, and your influence. Involvement in church is a two-way street of giving and receiving. Mature followers of Jesus graduate from "sitting and soaking" to "serving and giving." Church is a conduit for sharing Christ and growing in God's grace. Church provides accountability to Almighty God.

Christ is ever building His church to overcome sin, Satan, sorrow, and death. Jesus said, "I tell you that you are Peter, and on this rock I will build my church, and the gates of Hades will not overcome it" (Matthew 16:18). Do you value the church as Jesus values the church? Is church engagement a regular part of your routine? Meet God at church on Sunday to make Him known throughout the week.

———— ∞ ————

"[The church] was strengthened. Living in the
fear of the Lord and encouraged by the Holy
Spirit, it increased in numbers" (Acts 9:31).

How can I support my local church with my time and money?

Related Readings
Isaiah 25:1-9; John 3:29; 1 Corinthians 14:26; 2 Corinthians 11:2

An Angel of God

⟨⟩

*I saw an angel standing in the sun, who cried in a
loud voice to all the birds flying in midair, "Come,
gather together for the great supper of God."*

REVELATION 19:17

There is angelic activity in the unseen world of spiritual activity. These creations of God carry spiritual significance in your life, as they serve as God's messengers and His protectors. Do you look for evidence of angelic work around you? Have you considered that Christ has created your circumstances for His greater purpose? We know Jesus had thousands of angels at His side waiting to engage the enemy: "Do you think I cannot call on my Father, and he will at once put at my disposal more than twelve legions of angels?" (Matthew 26:53).

There are good and bad angels that vie for your attention. Once an angelic emissary presented itself to God, but Satan was in the mix: "One day the angels came to present themselves before the LORD, and Satan also came with them" (Job 1:6). Demons seek to accuse and destroy you with lies, while angels from the Lord lace their language with truth and hope. What voice do you hear when you feel pressure and fear? God's angel helped Joseph overcome his fears by assuring him that the Holy Spirit was the Creator of his circumstances.

⟨⟩

"An angel of the Lord appeared to him in a dream and
said, 'Joseph son of David, do not be afraid to take

Mary home as your wife, because what is conceived
in her is from the Holy Spirit'" (Matthew 1:20).

Angels offer confidence and security that Christ is in control. Take comfort in knowing that the enemy is being engaged on your behalf by a superior force and firepower. Use the Bible as your weapon of choice, and Satan and his demons will cringe and retreat at the sight of truth. Indeed, look out for and listen to the angelic voices in others.

Thank God for your guardian angels, but do not take them for granted or use them as an excuse for foolish behavior. "For he will command his angels concerning you to guard you in all your ways" (Psalm 91:11). Reckless living is not an excuse for the deployment of heavenly help. The devil attempted to lure Jesus into presuming on His heavenly Father's favor during a time of weakness, but He resisted him with Scripture. Angels are at the Almighty's disposal to come to your aid.

<hr>

"Jesus said to him, 'Away from me, Satan! For it is
written: "Worship the Lord your God, and serve
him only."' Then the devil left him, and angels
came and attended him" (Matthew 4:10-11).

Do I lean into the Lord, His Word, and angelic support when confronting Satan?

Related Readings
Genesis 19:15; Psalm 78:49; Matthew 13:49; Acts 23:8

81

Destination of Evildoers

⸺⸘⸺

*The beast was captured, and with it the false
prophet... The two of them were thrown
alive into the fiery lake of burning sulfur.*

REVELATION 19:20

The sun never sets on evil, and alarmingly, some people are as intent on evil actions as some are committed to good. Like roaches under the cloak of darkness, hideous human hearts are secretly hatching evil schemes. The worst kind of evil hides beneath the robe of religion. They blame their terrorist tirades on a god of their making. They worship an idol of violence at the altars of racism, anger, grudges, and hatred. These religious fanatics are deceived and delusional.

Satan smiles at acts of atrocity aimed at innocent people. When Satan convinces people to murder in the name of religion, he is executing a strategy for hell—sending people to hell for eternity and causing others to experience hell on earth. It is a hellish nightmare, the antithesis of true religion, and it is plaguing more and more of the modern world. Unfortunately, engineers of evil are engaged every day in the execution of evil acts. However, there is an unseen battle raging that is even more decisive—the battle for the souls of men and women.

⸺⸘⸺

"The LORD said to me, 'Son of man, these are
the men who are plotting evil and giving
wicked advice in this city'" (Ezekiel 11:2).

A person who comes to Christ in confession and repentance does not condemn others who hold different beliefs. People who are in Christ have new weapons in their arsenal of faith. Hate gives way to love. Violence gives way to peace. Death gives way to life. Retaliation gives way to forgiveness. Prayer is the primary weapon in spiritual warfare. Our friends in the faith who suffer under the tyranny of terrorism need our constant prayer support.

Until evil is totally transformed by the grace of God, we have a giant opportunity to invest in eternity. We have the remedy for radical religion driven by evil intent—faith in Christ. Humbly and persistently we can present Jesus in our behavior and in our beliefs. He is the answer for atrocities hatched in hell. Heaven trumps hell when trust in Christ is preeminent. Pray every day for trust in Christ to triumph over tactics of terrorism. Pray for His kingdom to come.

"Mark this: There will be terrible times in the last days. People will be lovers of themselves, lovers of money, boastful, proud, abusive, disobedient to their parents, ungrateful, unholy…having a form of godliness but denying its power. Have nothing to do with such people" (2 Timothy 3:1-2,5).

What areas of my heart have anger or hurt that may be hindering my relationships?

Related Readings
Jeremiah 14:14; Ezekiel 13:9; Mark 13:22; 2 Peter 2:1

82

Christ's Second Coming

They came to life and reigned with Christ a thousand years. (The rest of the dead did not come to life until the thousand years were ended.) This is the first resurrection.

REVELATION 20:4-5

Jesus came the first time in a modest manger to save the people from their sin. He was not the king, but He threatened the king's reign. Jesus is soon coming a second time with a grand entrance as King of kings to judge the people for their sin and dead works. He rode the first time on a humble donkey, but He will ride this second time on a brazen horse. This is the first resurrection.

Christ's second coming must matter most to the church because we are His bride, the body of Christ. How can the church be ready to greet its godly groom, Jesus? Like any faithful wife whose husband is away traveling for work or waging war overseas, we want to greet Him with a holy kiss. A faithful church is not conformed to the culture; rather, it transforms the culture. The faithful bride of Christ is ready to rejoice at His glorious sight!

"May he strengthen your hearts so that you will
be blameless and holy in the presence of our
God and Father when our Lord Jesus comes
with all his holy ones" (1 Thessalonians 3:13).

When Christ comes back He wants to catch the church evangelizing the lost and making disciples. He hungers for her disputes to be with the devil and not with each other. A humble church does not use finances to build man's kingdom, but instead deploys resources to advance the kingdom of God. The church is ready for Christ's return when she serves the poor, ministers to the community, prays for the sick, and preaches the gospel!

Christ's coming is also compelling for individual Christians. We want to be about our Lord's business and not preoccupied with activities and assets that will burn up one day. The judgment seat of Christ is for Christians—not to be judged for salvation, but to be judged for the quality of their works. You are wise when you invest in eternal matters with your time and money. Christlike character, missions, prayer, Bible teaching, corporate and individual worship, and service in the community all make Jesus smile. When Christ comes, make sure He catches you about your Father's business.

———∞———

"This is my prayer: that your love may abound more and more in knowledge and depth of insight, so that you may be able to discern what is best and may be pure and blameless for the day of Christ" (Philippians 1:9-10).

How can my church and I personally get ready for the second coming of Christ?

Related Readings
Ecclesiastes 12:14; Matthew 23:13; 1 Corinthians 3:9-15; 4:5

83

Death with Dignity

*I saw the dead, great and small, standing before
the throne, and books were opened.*

REVELATION 20:12

Death is imminent, but for some it comes sooner rather than later. So, have I put my house in order? The Lord wants me to think through the needs of my family, the state of my soul, and the glory I've brought Him in the process. It is death with dignity. The process is not without pain, but thinking through the practical issues that affect my loved ones and me is responsible.

Death is a transition. It is the end of trusting the unseen and the beginning of resting in God.

Think about your relationships. Are they whole? Maybe you need to ask someone for their forgiveness, or maybe you need to forgive them. Moreover, love your spouse and children by allowing God's Word to flow through you to them. Let them see your faith in action so that their faith becomes galvanized and grounded in Christ. Allow them to love you as you love them back—freely and passionately. Love like the Lord—always.

"'Where, O death, is your victory? Where, O
death, is your sting?' The sting of death is sin,
and the power of sin is the law. But thanks be

to God! He gives us the victory through our
Lord Jesus Christ" (1 Corinthians 15:55-57).

Talk about your funeral with those who care for you. What Scripture do you want read? What praise songs and hymns do you want sung? Death is a celebration of life on earth and a graduation to life eternal. Plan your funeral celebration as a graduation to glory. Prepare to die, and you are prepared to live. Use death as an excuse to point people to Jesus.

Most importantly, make right your relationship with God. Have you made peace with God? The foundation of your final preparation is your relationship with your heavenly Father. Let Him love and comfort you with His presence as you plan for the end. Put your house in order with your finances, family, friends, and faith. Die with dignity.

"Since we have been justified through faith, we have
peace with God through our Lord Jesus Christ,
through whom we have gained access by faith into
this grace in which we now stand. And we boast in
the hope of the glory of God" (Romans 5:1-2).

"This is what the LORD says: Put your house
in order, because you are going to die;
you will not recover" (2 Kings 20:1).

Is my house in order? What preparations do I need to make before I go to heaven?

Related Readings
Genesis 27:1-3; 2 Samuel 1:23; John 21:19; Romans 8:37-39

84

Eternal Rewards

⏤⏤ ∞∞∞ ⏤⏤

The dead were judged according to what
they had done as recorded in the books.

REVELATION 20:12

Those saved by grace and faith in Jesus are eternally secure, but eternal rewards are based on a disciple's efforts on earth. Believers who ignore their spiritual opportunities and obligations will miss out on their heavenly Father's affirmation and remuneration. Sober saints who take their Savior's expectations seriously will enter into the joy of their Master. Christ rewards obedience to Him.

Rewards in heaven are meant to be godly motivation. Yes, our first response is to serve Jesus out of love and our overflowing gratitude for His goodness and grace. Wise Christians fear the Lord and allow their holy awe of the Almighty to be foundational for their lives of faith and good works. But there is an end in mind: Jesus wants His children to be devoted and compelled by anticipating His generous gifts.

⏤⏤ ∞∞∞ ⏤⏤

"Without faith it is impossible to please God,
because anyone who comes to him must
believe that he exists and that he rewards those
who earnestly seek him" (Hebrews 11:6).

The process of renewing your mind with an eternal decision-making filter facilitates biblical thinking and doing. Ask the Lord in prayer how He wants you to invest your life in others. How does God want you to use your experience, your assets, your time, your money, and your influence for His purposes? In other words, how can you make eternal investments on earth that will bear fruit for God's glory—forever?

What you do does not get you to heaven; salvation comes only by faith in Christ and God's amazing grace. But what you do after becoming a follower of Jesus does determine the quality of your eternal experience. The persecuted and martyred in this life have a great reward waiting in the next life. Those who initiate resources and influence on behalf of the poor and needy bring great satisfaction to Jesus, which He expresses through bountiful blessings. Indeed, He rewards all those who diligently seek Him by faith.

Love God and your reward will be great. Be a faithful witness who plants or waters the gospel of Jesus Christ, and you will be rewarded by spending forever with eternally grateful souls. Send your investments ahead to heaven by aggressively giving yourself away on earth. Reject rewards from the culture so you are positioned to receive Christ's rewards. Remain faithful to God's call and look forward to His reward.

"[Moses] regarded disgrace for the sake of Christ as of greater value than the treasures of Egypt, because he was looking ahead to his reward" (Hebrews 11:26).

How can I live my life in a way that honors the Lord and looks forward to His rewards?

Related Readings

Amos 6:1-7; Matthew 16:27; Revelation 2:7-10; 22:12

85

Mystery of God Solved

———— ∞∞ ————

Then I saw "a new heaven and a new earth," for
the first heaven and the first earth had passed
away, and there was no longer any sea.

REVELATION 21:1

R ita and I like to create fun and interesting family gatherings, so
our children and grandchildren can't wait to get together. Easter
is one of the best times of the year because our family celebrates Jesus's
resurrection at church in worshipful celebration and at our home with
a feast and activities. One tradition is an Easter egg hunt using plastic
eggs with money inside. One golden egg holds $50! The coined eggs
are within eyesight, but the dollar-filled pastel ovals are hidden. After
many hints from Pop (me), the golden-egg mystery is solved.

The apostle John describes a new heaven and a new earth devoid of
any sea. What does he mean by "there was no longer any sea"? The sea
may be a symbol of the unknown, a mystery on earth that struck fear
in mostly land-hugging Jews who saw the sea as an untamed, raging
force that could destroy. Like the distant horizon, we only see the mystery of God through dimmed, human limitations. But a new, grander
elevation of wisdom accompanies those who go to be with the Lord. In
heaven the mystery of God is solved by being with God.

———— ∞∞ ————

"I am going to tell you a mystery—something
you may have trouble understanding: we will

not all fall asleep in death, but we will all be
transformed!" (1 Corinthians 15:51 VOICE).

Some mysterious questions will remain unanswered until we get to
heaven. Why did my godly friend die so young with such a large, loving family left behind? What exactly are eternal rewards? How does the
Trinity love one another? Why must Jesus come to earth twice? Why
did Jesus and why do Christians suffer deep pain?

We must be comfortable with the unknown because we are the creatures, not the Creator. The mystery of the Lord, the church, and the
gospel has already been solved, though we still wait for eternal understanding. The Holy Spirit shows us just what we need to know, just in
time. If we knew too much too soon, we might become proud or lazy
in our faith. In the meantime, we investigate and trust Christ—God's
best clue to divine mystery.

"He made known to us the mystery of his
will according to his good pleasure, which
he purposed in Christ" (Ephesians 1:9).

What about God do I need to leave in His hands? How can I
develop my trust in Him, believing He knows what's best for
me and others?

Related Readings

Isaiah 48:6; Romans 16:25; Ephesians 3:3-6; Colossians 1:26;
1 Timothy 3:16

86

God's Dwelling Place

*Look! God's dwelling place is now among
the people, and he will dwell with them.*

REVELATION 21:3

With millions of dollars, one can design and build a luxury resort fully adorned with exotic spas, private pools, the finest of foods, and a service experience full of adult pampering. Human attempts to create environments that exclude any angst or effort are temporary at best. Like Cinderella—who experienced a magical evening with the prince at his palace—we eventually must go back to the real world. Fortunately for followers of Jesus, there is eternal extravagance to anticipate. Heaven is more than absence of sin—it is the presence of God, His dwelling place.

John's description of heaven depicts the Old Testament tabernacle as God's dwelling place, a place of worship. But instead of limiting access to priests, God allows all who worship Jesus, the great High Priest, to visit His dwelling place. In heaven the purified bride of Christ—His church—is qualified to experience the pure presence of the Lord at all times. He dwells with heaven's inhabitants, and they dwell with Him. Christ dwells with His children on earth, but one day His children will dwell with Him in heaven: perpetual, perfect, and pure!

"I pray that out of his glorious riches he may
strengthen you with power through his Spirit

in your inner being, so that Christ may dwell in
your hearts through faith" (Ephesians 3:16-17).

Is Jesus at home in your heart? Does He have access to all aspects
of your life? Genuine faith permeates your relationships, finances, free
time, and work. The heart is the Holy Spirit's haven. Sin is not comfortable or welcome in a heart where the Spirit takes sanctuary. Fear flees a
faith-filled heart, established in love. You may wonder, "What are my
priorities? How do I balance all that needs to get done?" Start by invit-
ing the Holy Spirit's fullness into your heart.

When we fully experience Christ dwelling in our hearts, we are able
to glimpse what it will be like to dwell with God in heaven. Our imperfect love will be perfected by the perfect love of the Lamb—Jesus. Our
hurried worship will be transformed into unhurried worship with the
angels in the holy city. God's dwelling place is the destination of broken people in search of heaven's wholeness. A heart for Christ keeps a
constant eye toward dwelling together forever.

"If Christ is in you, then even though your body is
subject to death because of sin, the Spirit gives
life because of righteousness" (Romans 8:10).

What suffering soul can I encourage with anticipation of their
eternal dwelling?

Related Readings
Exodus 29:45; John 14:20; 2 Corinthians 13:5;
Colossians 1:27; 3:16

87

Good List

⁓

Nothing impure will ever enter it, nor will anyone who does what is shameful or deceitful, but only those whose names are written in the Lamb's book of life.

REVELATION 21:27

God keeps a record in the Lamb's book of life of those who have trusted His Son Jesus as their Lord and Savior. Salvation from hell to heaven begs the questions, "Is my name written in the book of life? Am I on the good list?" Yes, if you believe Jesus died for your sins and rose from the grave to give you life in Him, you are known in heaven. There is a required transaction of faith in Jesus before you can enjoy sweet fellowship with Jesus. God's good list offers eternal security.

Believers in Jesus do not receive a final judgment of separation from God. When you welcome His presence on earth, God will not exclude you from His presence in heaven. However, there is a judgment after death for Christians regarding how they behaved in this life. Did we store up treasures in heaven, or did we waste our time with the trinkets of earth? Joyous will be followers of Jesus who bow before their Lord and hear Him say, "Well done!"

⁓

"Their work will be shown for what it is, because the [Judgment] Day will bring it to light. It will be revealed with fire, and the fire will test the quality of each person's work" (1 Corinthians 3:13).

By God's grace we seek to be righteous in this brief life, for this is the caliber of our eternal life. Assurance of being on the good list is not an excuse to live for the flesh; rather, our salvation offers freedom and motivation to live for the spirit. Our corruptible flesh will perish, but our incorruptible spirit will live. An individual who chooses heaven over hell desires a heavenly quality of life. The Holy Spirit within yearns for holiness without. Love wins when our name is in His book.

Rejoice because your Savior never ever uses an eraser. He writes your name in stone. Just as the government records your physical birthday, so heaven records your spiritual date of birth. It is well with your soul, since your salvation is sealed by the Holy Spirit. You are on the good list, so do good with God. Invite others to stand firm in Christ Jesus!

"He anointed us, set his seal of ownership on us, and put his Spirit in our hearts as a deposit, guaranteeing what is to come" (2 Corinthians 1:21-22).

Heavenly Father, thank You that through the blood of Your Son Jesus, my name is forever written in the Lamb's book of life.

Related Readings

Psalm 69:28; Philippians 4:3; 2 Thessalonians 1:7; Hebrews 2:3

88

Work as Worship

*The throne of God and of the Lamb will be in
the city, and his servants will serve him.*

REVELATION 22:3-4

My work is so much more than a job. A job is for making money. A job keeps me busy. A job makes me a productive citizen. A job provides for my family. My work, on the other hand, is worship of Almighty God, my Savior and Lord. Work is a doxology of what God is up to in my life and in the lives of those I serve. A point to parse: Work is not to be worshipped, but it is part of my worship.

John does not describe our heavenly work as a curse. Serving our Savior, the Lamb of God, is a gift and a blessing. God cursed the dirt and condemned Adam to laborious toil because he failed to trust God and disobeyed His only command. But in heaven our work is restful, and our rest is serving others. The loving face of Christ is what the saints see during their worshipful work. His name on their foreheads is a symbol of a life branded by the Lord.

"I urge you, brothers and sisters, in view of
God's mercy, to offer your bodies as a living
sacrifice, holy and pleasing to God—this is your
true and proper worship" (Romans 12:1).

Don't spend your life in joyless service. Seek to serve with heartfelt gratitude to God, and joy will return to your work. Worship Jesus as you walk around at work with a smile on your face. Worship Jesus with focused intensity, as you seek to solve a problem or support a team member. Worship Jesus with a loud laugh, a quiet thank-you, or an appropriate prayer over a hurting heart. Worship as you work, and work as you worship!

Rest from your work is necessary for a clear mind, healthy emotions, a motivated spirit, and an energized body. Rest well on your weekly Sabbath and your much-needed days off. Also, don't miss your opportunity to rest while you work. Yes, you are liberated to labor with added inner stamina, as your work is worship to the Lord. Love invigorates. Love revives. Love refreshes. Love rejuvenates. Love gives. Loves serves. Love rests in its work as it worships Jesus as Lord!

"They exchanged the truth about God for a lie, and worshiped and served created things rather than the Creator—who is forever praised. Amen" (Romans 1:25).

What are everyday ways I can work as worship to Jesus Christ?

Related Readings
Job 36:24; Psalm 103:22; Joel 2:26; Colossians 3:23-24; Hebrews 12:28

89

Face Time with Jesus

*No longer will there be any curse…They will see
his face, and his name will be on their foreheads.*

REVELATION 22:3-4

Some things are best communicated face-to-face. A proposal for marriage, a job interview, a mentor relationship, family time, explaining an issue, showing appreciation…all these thrive in a one-on-one relational environment. Fear tends to force us away from direct engagement with people. We sometimes avoid human contact because of overwhelming insecurity, fear of rejection, or busyness. The seasons of face time with our families are gone before we know it. Our children are off with friends, attending college, and then married. Face time in the moment means the most now.

By faith, the eyes of our soul need to gaze at God. If we chronically miss coming alongside Christ, we burn out in our own strength. We desperately need face time, by faith, with Jesus. We need His affirmation and love, we need His instruction and correction, we need His warm embrace, and we need His discernment and wisdom. It is imperative that we spend daily time in prayer and in studying God's Word, absorbing it into our minds and hearts. Regular face time with God in Scripture is what transforms our thinking with truth.

"I have much to write to you, but I do not want
to use paper and ink. Instead, I hope to visit

you and talk with you face to face, so that
our joy may be complete" (2 John 12).

Schedule time daily, weekly, monthly, and yearly with those you love. Invest time and money in face time with your son, your daughter, your spouse, your parents, and your friends. Face time lets you see the fear in their eyes and extend encouragement toward them. Face time lets your smile shine a ray of hope across a discouraged heart. Face time is your opportunity to discuss hard issues and be sure the sincerity of your love is not missed.

You can tell when someone has been with Jesus. They have peace that brings calm; they have patience that extends a second chance; they have boldness based on wisdom; they have love that forgives; they have service that is relentless; they have faith that is strong; they have hope that perseveres. Thus, invest time in your relationship with the Almighty. Keep an eye on eternity, for one day you will see Jesus face-to-face—forever!

<hr />

"The LORD would speak to Moses face to face,
as one speaks to a friend" (Exodus 33:11).

How can I keep my gaze on eternity and my glance on the temporal?

Related Readings
Genesis 33:10; Job 33:26; 2 Corinthians 4:6; Hebrews 12:1-3

90

Access to the City of God

⟨≈≈⟩

Blessed are those who wash their robes, that
they may have the right to the tree of life and
may go through the gates into the city.

REVELATION 22:14

Years ago as a young minister, my friend Andy Stanley came by my office at his dad's church and asked if I wanted to meet Billy Graham. Taken aback and totally humbled, I stammered out a whispered yes, quickly followed by an exuberant "Absolutely!" The occasion was a pastor's reception prior to one of Dr. Graham's Sunday night crusades. When we arrived at the Georgia Dome, which was buzzing with activity, a team member took us to meet Billy along with other ministry leaders. I had access to a moment with Mr. Graham because of Dr. Stanley's character and credibility.

John describes the last beatitude given by Jesus. Those whose character is cleansed by Christ are qualified to access God's presence here and in heaven. Blackened garments soiled by sin but washed in the sanitizing salvation of Jesus's blood create a new and beautiful creation—radiant white, purified by the grace of God. Through eternal life, the tree of life is accessible—with blessings unknown to earthly pilgrims still on their journey of faith. The Garden in Genesis and the City of God in Revelation are the two bookends of Creation; and all who are redeemed—between the beginning and the end of time—may worship God forever.

"For through him we both have access to the
Father by one Spirit" (Ephesians 2:18).

The relationships you invest in now are most likely the relationships God uses to open doors in the future. Treat all individuals with love and concern, for God may have set them in your path. Be more motivated to bless than to be blessed, and the blessings you need will come.

Most importantly, enjoy full access to your heavenly Father. He is intimate with His children who walk in integrity. Your imperfect character has access to the Lord's perfection. Bring your brokenness and access Christ's healing. Bring your pride and access God's humility. Bring your weaknesses and access the Spirit's strength. Ultimately, it's the character and credibility of Christ that gives you unquestionable access to the throne of God's grace. As often as you breathe and eat, seek communion with Christ. Through faith, access the riches of His grace.

"God raised us up with Christ and seated us with him in
the heavenly realms in Christ Jesus" (Ephesians 2:6).

What opportunity am I praying about that requires the elevation of my character?

Related Readings
Romans 5:1-5; Ephesians 2:17-19; 3:12; Hebrews 7:18-21;
1 John 5:14

How to Become a Disciple of Jesus Christ

———— ∞∞∞ ————

*Then Jesus came to them and said, "All authority in
heaven and on earth has been given to me. Therefore
go and make disciples of all nations, baptizing
them in the name of the Father and of the Son
and of the Holy Spirit, and teaching them to obey
everything I have commanded you. And surely I
am with you always, to the very end of the age."*

MATTHEW 28:18-20

Holy Scripture teaches us how to become disciples and how to make disciples.

Believe

Belief in Jesus Christ as your Savior and Lord gives you eternal life in heaven.

> If you declare with your mouth, "Jesus is Lord," and believe in your heart that God raised him from the dead, you will be saved (Romans 10:9).

Repent and Be Baptized

To repent is to turn from your sin and then publicly confess Christ in baptism.

> Repent and be baptized, every one of you, in the name of Jesus Christ for the forgiveness of your sins. And you will receive the gift of the Holy Spirit (Acts 2:38).

Obey

Obedience is an indicator of our love for the Lord Jesus and His presence in our life.

> Jesus replied, "Anyone who loves me will obey my teaching. My Father will love them, and we will come to them and make our home with them" (John 14:23).

Worship, Prayer, Community, Evangelism, and Study

Worship and prayer express our gratitude and honor to God and our dependence on His grace. Community and evangelism show our accountability to Christians and compassion for non-Christians. We study to apply the knowledge, understanding, and wisdom of God.

> Every day they continued to meet together in the temple courts. They broke bread in their homes and ate together with glad and sincere hearts, praising God and enjoying the favor of all the people. And the Lord added to their number daily those who were being saved (Acts 2:46-47).

Love God

Intimacy with Almighty God is a growing and loving relationship. We are loved by Him, so we can love others and be empowered by the Holy Spirit to obey His commands.

> Jesus replied: "'Love the Lord your God with all your heart and with all your soul and with all your mind.' This is the first and greatest commandment" (Matthew 22:37-38).

Love People

Our love for others flows from our love for our heavenly Father. We are able to love because He first loved us.

> And the second is like it: "Love your neighbor as yourself" (Matthew 22:39).

Make Disciples

We disciple others because we are grateful to God and to those who disciple us, and we want to obey Christ's last instructions before going to heaven.

> The things you have heard me say in the presence of many witnesses entrust to reliable people who will also be qualified to teach others (2 Timothy 2:2).

About the Author

Boyd Bailey is the president of the National Christian Foundation (NCF) Georgia. His passion is to encourage followers of Jesus to grow in their faith by being generous givers with their time, money, resources, and relationships.

Since 2004, Boyd has also served as president and founder of Wisdom Hunters, a ministry that connects people to Christ through devotional writing, with more than 100,000 daily email readers.

In 1999 Boyd cofounded Ministry Ventures, which has trained approximately 1000 faith-based nonprofits and coached for certification more than 200 ministries in the best practices of prayer, board development, ministry model, administration, and fundraising. By God's grace, these ministries have raised more than $100 million, and thousands of people have been led into growing relationships with Jesus Christ.

Prior to Ministry Ventures, Boyd was the national director for Crown Financial Ministries. He was instrumental in the expansion of Crown into 30 major markets across the United States. He was a key facilitator in the $25 million merger between Christian Financial Concepts and Crown Ministries.

Before his work with Crown, Boyd and Andy Stanley started First Baptist Atlanta's north campus, and as an elder, Boyd assisted Andy in the start of North Point Community Church.

Boyd received a bachelor of arts from Jacksonville State University and a master's of divinity from Southwestern Seminary in Fort Worth, Texas. Boyd and his wife, Rita, live in Roswell, Georgia. They have been married 34 years and are blessed with four daughters, three sons-in-law, and five grandchildren.

Wisdom Hunters

"Walk with the wise and become wise, for a companion of fools suffers harm" (Proverbs 13:20).

In 2003, Boyd Bailey began to informally email personal reflections from his morning devotional time to a select group of fellow wisdom hunters. Over time, these informal emails grew into Wisdom Hunters Daily Devotional. Today, thanks to God's favor and faithful followers, these emails and social media posts reach more than 150,000 readers each morning.

We remain relentless in the pursuit of wisdom and continue to daily write raw, original, real-time reflections from our personal encounters with the Lord. Visit **WisdomHunters.com**, where you can...

- Subscribe to free daily devotional emails
- Find out how to follow us on Facebook, Twitter, Instagram, our blog, and the new Wisdom Hunters podcast
- Download the free Wisdom Hunters app for Apple and Android
- Choose from a wide selection of devotional books on marriage, wisdom, wise living, fatherhood, and more (ebook and print versions available)

The National Christian Foundation

Founded in 1982 and based in Atlanta, Georgia, the National Christian Foundation (NCF) is a charitable giving ministry that provides wise giving solutions, mobilizes resources, and inspires biblical generosity with Christian families, advisors, and charities. NCF is currently the ninth-largest US nonprofit, having accepted more than $9 billion in contributions and granted more than $7 billion to more than 40,000 charities. The NCF Giving Fund, or donor-advised fund, allows donors to make charitable contributions and then recommend grants to the charities they care about over time. NCF is also an industry leader in accepting gifts of appreciated assets, such as stocks, real estate, and business interests, which enables donors to save taxes and align their charitable goals with their family, business, estate, and legacy plans. Learn more about NCF at **www.ncfgiving.com**.

More Great Harvest House Devotionals
by Boyd Bailey

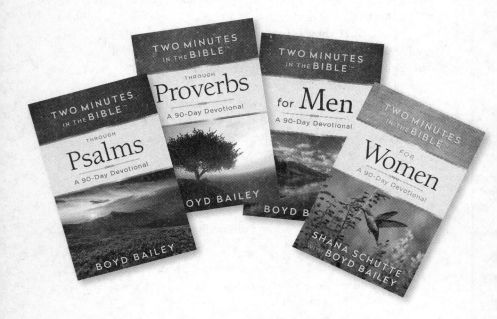

To learn more about Harvest House books and
to read sample chapters, visit our website:

www.harvesthousepublishers.com

HARVEST HOUSE PUBLISHERS
EUGENE, OREGON

Trouble at sea

AUTHOR

Waring, jamall

TITLE

Amanda/ED

DATE DUE	BORROWER'S NAME	ROOM NUMBER
10-23-07	wilber loeza	per.2

DATE DUE	BORROWER'S NAME	ROOM NUMBER
		PRINTED IN U.S.A.